Bryan Stephens

Meetings in English

Be effective in international meetings

Macmillan Education Limited
4 Crinan Street
London N1 9XW
Companies and representatives throughout the world

ISBN 978-0-230-40190-7

Text © Bryan Stephens 2011
Design and illustration © Macmillan Education Limited 2011

First published 2011

All rights reserved; no part of this publication may be reproduced, stored in a retrieval system, transmitted in any form, or by any means, electronic, mechanical, photocopying, recording, or otherwise, without the prior written permission of the publishers.

Book design by Anthony Godber
Page make-up by Anne Davies
Illustrated by eMC Design and Gary Wing
Cover design by Andrew Oliver
Cover photograph by Photodisk

Author's acknowledgements:
The author would like to thank Evgenia Myasoedova for her love, endless support, crucial feedback and inspiration during the whole project. He also thanks his boys, William and Gregory, who at the tender age of two, unwittingly showed great patience when their dad was too busy to play with them.

The author and publishers would like to thank the following for permission to reproduce their photographic material:

Arts Photo Library p70(c); Bananastock pp6(bml), 18(cr), 18(cr), 18(br) 53(bl), 53(bm), 27(tml), 38(bmr), 45(tl), 53(bl), 53(bm), 67(bl), 69(cr), 84(tm); Brand X pp22(cmr), 23(tmr), 27(tl), p61(cr); Bryan Stephens / Evgenia Myasoedova p56(cmr); Christopher Furlong/staff p70(cmr); Corbis pp6(cl), 6(bmr), 10(tr), 18(bmr), 21(cmr), 22(cmr), 32(cmr), 39(tmr), 64(br), 70(cml), 72(bmr), 84(tr); Chris L Jones p50(tmr); Comstock p53(br); Coll Lisette Le Bon p55(cr); Creatas p23(tr); Digital Vision p27(tm); Florian Franke p42(cmr); Getty pp6(c), 6(cr), 18(cr), 18(cmr), 18(br), 21(cml), 21(c), 26 (cr), 28(c), 38(cr), 45(tr), 45(cl), 45(cr), 47(tr), 58(tr), 69(cr) 75(tr), 84(tl); Image Source pp14(tmr), 27(tmr), 42(cml) 56(cr), 63(tl), 71(cmr), 76(cr), 79(tr); Image 100 p84(cml); Kablonk p81(cr); Macmillan Australia pp6(tl), 18(cmr), 18(bmr); Macmillan English Dictionary p4(br); Macmillan Mexico / Andy Keylock p66(tr); Macmillan / Paul Bricknell / Dean Ryan p23(cmr); Ojo Images pp30(cr), 42(cml); Photodisc pp23(cr), 60(tr); Rex Features pp30(cr), 42(cml); Rubber Ball p34(cr); Stockbyte pp11(cr), 13(tmr), 17(tr), 35(br), 39(cmr), 45(c); Superstock p46(cr).

These materials may contain links for third party websites. We have no control over, and are not responsible for, the contents of such third party websites. Please use care when accessing them.

Although we have tried to trace and contact copyright holders before publication, in some cases this has not been possible. If contacted we will be pleased to rectify any errors or omissions at the earliest opportunity.

All key word definitions taken from or based on the Macmillan English Dictionary © Macmillan Publishers 2007.

Printed and bound by CPI Group (UK) Ltd, Croydon CR0 4YY
2020
11 10 9 8

Contents

To the student and teacher	4
Inside a meeting room	5
Unit 1: Types of meeting	6
Unit 2: Arranging to meet	10
Unit 3: Writing emails in preparation for meetings	14
Unit 4: Confirming and rescheduling meetings	18
Unit 5: Booking a business centre for a meeting	22
Unit 6: Planning meetings	26
Unit 7: Networking before a meeting	30
Unit 8: Opening a meeting	34
Unit 9: Introducing yourself at a meeting	38
Unit 10: Moving through the agenda and summarizing the discussion	42
Unit 11: Opening a videoconference	46
Unit 12: Keeping the discussion on track	50
Unit 13: Coping with strong disagreement	54
Unit 14: Dealing fairly and sensitively with difficult issues	58
Unit 15: Taking part in a brainstorming meeting	62
Unit 16: Reporting back to the client	66
Unit 17: Ending a meeting	70
Unit 18: A formal board meeting	74
Unit 19: Writing the minutes	78
Unit 20: Monitoring action and evaluating meetings	82
Case studies	86
Useful language	94
Listening scripts	99
Answer key	107
Can do checklist	112

To the student and teacher

This book is for professional people and business English students who wish to improve their skills in meetings. It can be used by pre-intermediate students and above, in class or as a free-standing book for self-study.

Syllabus

The book offers systematic coverage of all aspects of meetings in English: the different types of meeting, arranging and preparing for meetings, socializing in and around meetings, managing and participating in discussions, and follow-up. Aiming to develop students' skills in all of these areas, the book consists of 20 units of four pages each. The first six units deal with organizing meetings, Unit 7 covers social networking before a meeting, Units 8 to 18 deal with managing and participating in both formal and informal meetings, and the last two units cover follow-up after meetings.

Course features

The book has a particular emphasis on vocabulary, listening and speaking, which form the absolute basis of successful communication in meetings. The audio CD allows students and teachers to listen to natural meeting scenarios, and to play and replay as desired. There is also a good deal of material to develop students' reading and writing skills, and each unit includes focused grammar and pronunciation practice.

Imaginary companies and characters add a real-life edge to the content. Some of these companies are the focus of two or more units; others appear just once. All are introduced in brief on their first appearance in the book. 'Culture points' also appear regularly throughout, emphasizing the importance of cultural sensitivity when participating in international meetings.

Each unit is divided up into four main sections: 'Background' gives company and cultural information relevant to the unit; 'Skills work' is the main part of the unit and focuses primarily on receptive skills (listening and reading) practice; 'Further practice' provides additional exercises in pronunciation, grammar and vocabulary; 'Over to you' gives students the chance to develop their speaking skills. Additional communicative activities can be found in the 'Case studies' section at the back of the book. These work best when the student refers to, and tries to put into practice, the relevant language in the 'Useful language' section, which lists phrases in useful categories for easy reference. There is also an answer key for all activities together with a copy of all recorded texts.

How to use this book

This book is very flexible and the units can be studied independently from each other. Students don't have to do all the units if they don't meet their personal needs – for example, they need not do Unit 18 if they never attend very formal meetings. On page 112 there is a 'Can do checklist', which maps the content of the book with practical 'I can…' statements. Students can refer to this checklist both before using the book (to find out which areas of meetings are most important and relevant to them) and afterwards (to highlight which areas they still need to work on). If there are any statements that the student cannot tick, then he/she should focus on those units.

If you are not studying in a class, you can work with the book and the audio CD. When you see a speaking activity you can prepare for it and then say it aloud for yourself. You can also use the 'Useful language' section at the end of the book to practise using the new language.

Further resources

For further practice with English grammar, *Intermediate Language Practice* by Michael Vince (Macmillan Publishers, 2010) is recommended.

The monolingual *Macmillan English Dictionary* (MED) is an excellent vocabulary resource for this level. An electronic version of the dictionary is available on the accompanying CD-ROM or the MED website (www.macmillandictionary.com). If you need help with your pronunciation, you can click on the icon next to a word and listen to the stress. Alternatively, you can practise saying the word using the microphone, and compare your pronunciation with the original.

Inside a meeting room

Unit 1 Types of meeting

Background

 Delta International is a language training company with over two hundred centres worldwide. Its head office and warehouse are in Lille, France, from which it distributes its teaching and marketing materials to the franchise owners.

Culture point – Decision-making Some cultures rely less on meetings, and in some countries top managers often make decisions without consulting or telling other members of staff. What is it like in your country? Do all workers have a say in the way their company is run?

Skills work

1 Listen to seven conversations. Who is telephoning who in each conversation? Draw a line and number between the caller and the receiver. The first one is done for you.

 **Rick Casbon**
Company President
Delta International

 **Uwe Timm**
Managing Director
Delta International

 **Jenny Tidman**
Project manager
Delta International

 **Paul Hoffman**
Design manager
Delta International

 **Tom Buddell**
IT manager
Softecco

2 Listen again and write the number of the correct conversation (1–7) next to each document opposite (a–g).

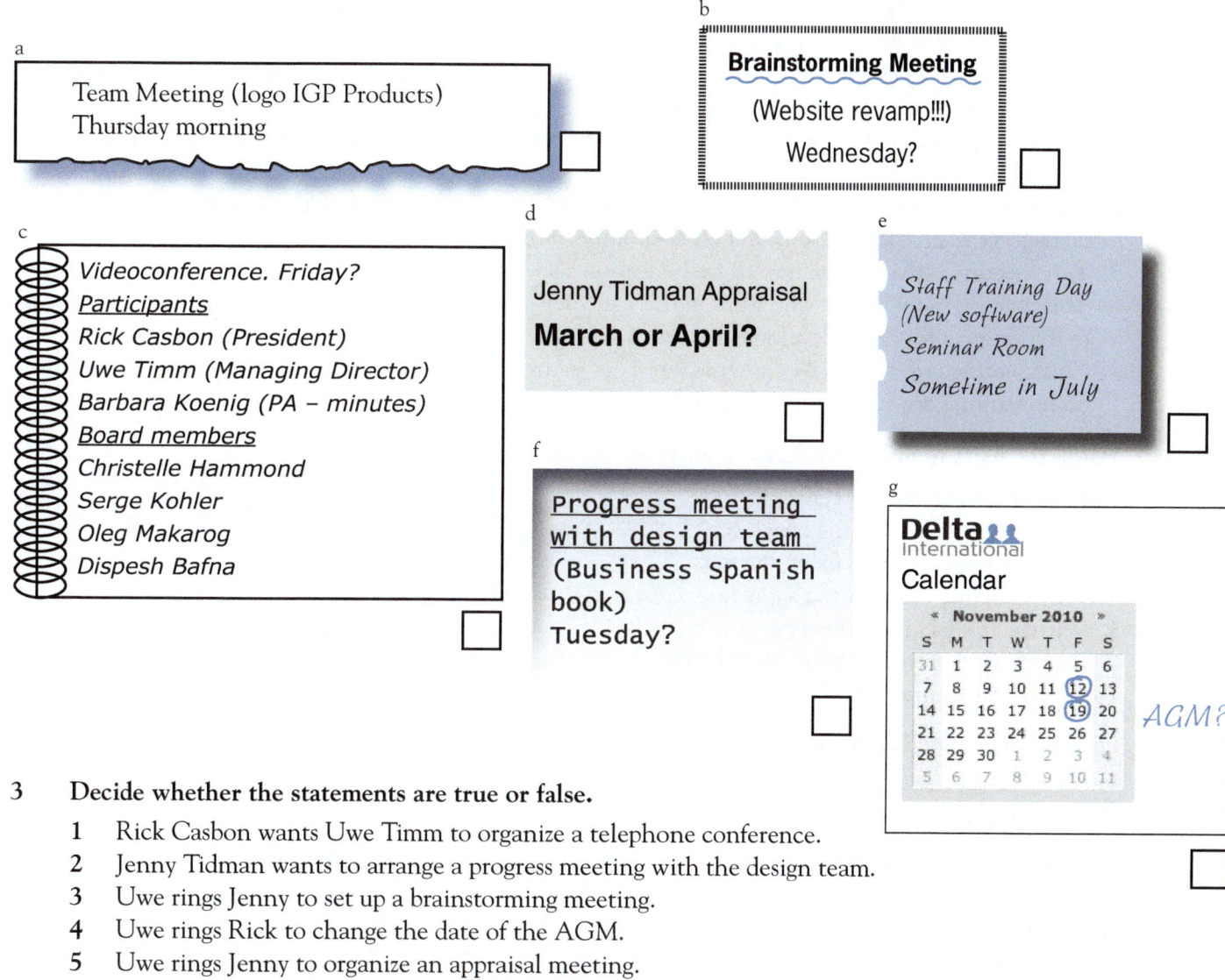

3 Decide whether the statements are true or false.

1 Rick Casbon wants Uwe Timm to organize a telephone conference.
2 Jenny Tidman wants to arrange a progress meeting with the design team.
3 Uwe rings Jenny to set up a brainstorming meeting.
4 Uwe rings Rick to change the date of the AGM.
5 Uwe rings Jenny to organize an appraisal meeting.
6 Jenny rings Paul to cancel a training meeting.

4 Read listening script 1 on page 99 to check your answers to exercise 3. Look up any words that you don't know.

5 Look at the different types of meetings in the table and read the descriptions on the next page. Complete the table with the number of the correct description (1–7). The first one is done for you.

Type of meeting	Description
annual general meeting (AGM)	
progress meeting	
board meeting	1
team meeting	
brainstorming meeting	
staff appraisal meeting	
training meeting	

Unit 1 Types of meeting

1 This is a meeting for company directors and top managers to discuss strategy and make decisions regarding the direction of a company.
2 This meeting is held once a year to give all members or shareholders information about the progress of the company in the past, present and future.
3 This meeting is to help employees to do their job better by teaching them new techniques or giving them new information.
4 This meeting gives individual staff the opportunity to discuss their work with their managers, and managers can give feedback to staff on their job performance.
5 This meeting is to generate new or fresh ideas on a specific topic.
6 This meeting is for people who work in the same department or section. The purpose of the meeting is to inform people of new developments and discuss the present situation.
7 This meeting is to help make sure that a project is on schedule. It is also an opportunity to get feedback on how things are going and to exchange ideas.

6 Match the pairs to make sentences about types of meetings.

1 I'm just calling about organizing
2 Is it possible to discuss the new logo
3 I was ringing to try and fix up the next
4 I was thinking of setting up a meeting to
5 We need to decide on the date
6 Do you think we could fix a date for your
7 I'd like to organize a training

a day on the new software.
b progress meeting.
c of the annual general meeting.
d annual appraisal?
e at our next team meeting?
f brainstorm ideas for the website.
g a videoconference.

For more on arranging to meet, see Unit 2.

Further practice

7 **Pronunciation practice.** Now listen to the sentences in 6 and repeat them.

> **Key words**
> **annual** (adjective): happening once a year
> **feedback** (noun): comments about how well or how badly someone is doing something
> **franchise** (noun): an agreement to sell a company's products, using the company's name
> **generate** (verb): to create

8 Prepositions. Fill in the gaps with the correct prepositions.

| through | for | up | at | on | with | about | of |

1 When can we fix _____ the meeting?
2 I'll put you _____ now.
3 We need to decide _____ the date.
4 Can we discuss that _____ the next meeting?
5 I'm organizing a videoconference _____ the board.
6 I'm just calling _____ your appraisal next week.
7 I was thinking _____ setting up a team meeting.
8 I want to arrange a meeting _____ members of the production team.

Unit 1 Types of meeting

Over to you

9 Prepare answers to these questions.
   1 How often do you go to meetings in English?
   2 What type of meetings do you go to in English and in your own language?

10 Now interview other students about the meetings they attend. Make a note of their answers and report back your findings. See the example below on the clipboard.

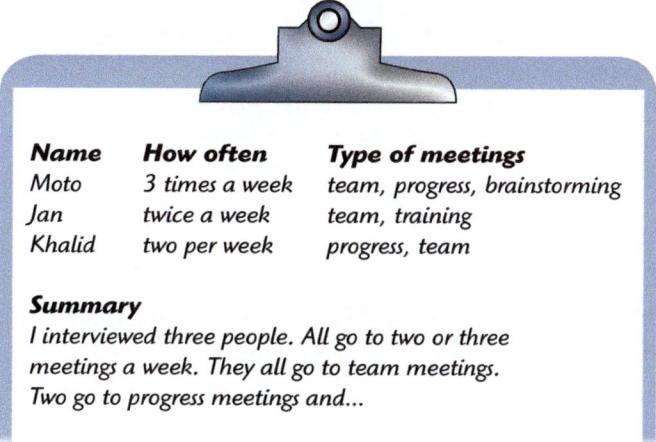

Name   **How often**   **Type of meetings**
Moto   3 times a week   team, progress, brainstorming
Jan   twice a week   team, training
Khalid   two per week   progress, team

Summary
I interviewed three people. All go to two or three meetings a week. They all go to team meetings. Two go to progress meetings and...

11 Without looking back at the unit, brainstorm different types of meetings with a partner. Complete the mind map with your ideas.

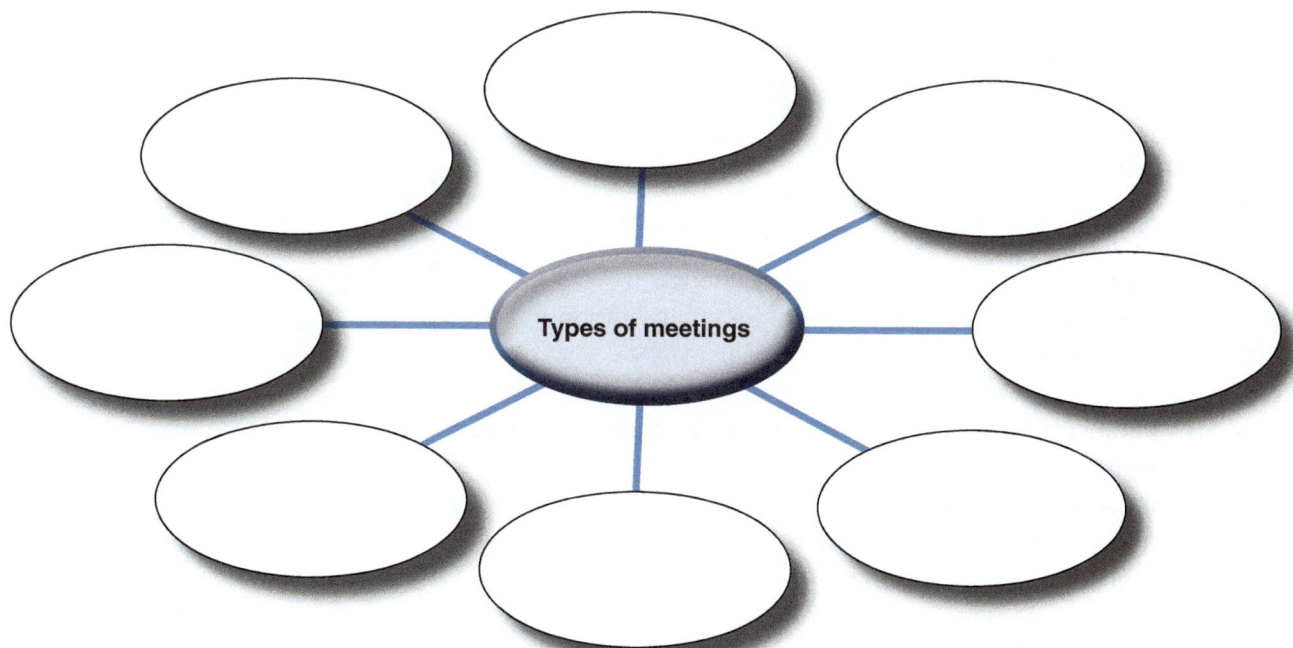

For more on brainstorming and mind maps, see Unit 15.

12 Now turn to Case study 1 on page 86 for practice on talking about different types of meetings.

13 For a list of expressions from this unit, see Useful language Unit 1 on page 94.

Unit 2 Arranging to meet

Background

In the last unit we looked at the different types of meetings that take place in companies like Delta International. It is now time to look more closely at how they are set up.

> *Culture point – Punctuality* In some cultures punctuality is very important, but in others being late for an appointment is not a big problem. In fact, in some cultures there are even acceptable degrees of lateness, so always ask for a mobile number! What would you say if somebody arrived 15/30/45/60 minutes late?

Skills work

1   Read the conversation below, in which Jenny Tidman from Delta International tries to arrange a progress meeting with Paul Hoffman and the design team. Then decide which spaces (1–7) the questions below (a–g) fit into. Write the correct number next to each question.

JENNY: Paul, have you got a minute?
PAUL: Yeah, sure.
JENNY: ___(1)___ We really need to check that everything is still on target.
PAUL: Sorry, that's not going be possible. I'm at the Frankfurt Book Fair for three days and then I was going to take a couple of days' leave.
JENNY: Oh, OK. ___(2)___
PAUL: Yeah, OK. ___(3)___
JENNY: Sorry, I'm out of the office on Monday.
PAUL: ___(4)___ I'm free all day.
JENNY: Great. ___(5)___
PAUL: That's fine. ___(6)___
JENNY: Yeah, that's perfect. ___(7)___
PAUL: I think a couple of hours should be enough.
JENNY: OK, sounds good. I'll send you a formal invitation in a bit.
PAUL: Thanks Jenny.

a   Could we try to arrange a progress meeting sometime next week? _____
b   How long do you think we'll need? _____
c   What about the following week then? _____
d   Shall we meet here in the design office as usual? _____
e   How about Monday morning? _____
f   How about after lunch – say two o'clock? _____
g   Sometime on Tuesday then? _____

2   Now practise saying the conversation.

3 🔊 Listen to some extracts from other phone calls made by the Delta International staff and complete the missing details in the table.

	Who?	What?	When?
1	Jenny Tidman/Paul Hoffman	Staff development meeting	
2	Uwe Timm/Rick Casbon		
3	Uwe Timm/Paul Hoffman		Thursday, 9.30–10.30am
4	Uwe Timm/Jenny Tidman	Brainstorming meeting	
5	Rick Casbon/Uwe Timm		
6	Uwe Timm/Jenny Tidman	Appraisal meeting	

4 Match the beginnings and endings to make questions about arranging meetings.

1 Could we schedule
2 Could we find
3 Is there any chance
4 Can we arrange to
5 What about a
6 Can you organize a conference
7 What date do
8 How about meeting

a meet sometime?
b in my office?
c a time to meet?
d of scheduling a meeting next week?
e you have in mind?
f a meeting sometime next month?
g meeting next Monday?
h call next month?

5 Make sentences to say you can/can't attend meetings. The first one is done for you.

1 can / I / make / date. / Yes, / that   *Yes, I can make that date.*
2 on / I'm / Yes, / free / date. / that
3 at / for / nine / Tuesday / o'clock / fine / is / me.
4 I / week. / can't / the / Sorry, / meeting / make / next
5 afraid / I'm / not, / I'm / on / away / a / trip. / business
6 o'clock / at / sounds / Wednesday / 15th / 11 / the / good.
7 sure, / Yes / about / Tuesday / how / Monday / 9th? / or / 8th
8 I'm / Yes, / happy / morning. / next / with / Monday
9 another / I / I'm / appointment / have / afraid / then.
10 Yes, / that / me. / date / for / works

Further practice

6  Pronunciation practice. Now listen to the sentences in 5 and repeat them.

> **Key words**
> **appointment** (noun): an arrangement to see someone at a particular time
> **leave** (noun): a period of time away from your job
> **schedule** (noun): a timetable, plan of activities and when they will happen
> **schedule** (verb): to plan something to happen at a particular time

Unit 2 Arranging to meet

7 **Present simple tense. Fill in the gaps with a word from the box.**

is   think   am   do   have   need   can

1 _____ I come and meet you and the team this week?
2 We really _____ to check that everything _____ still on target.
3 I _____ at the Frankfurt Book Fair for three days.
4 How long _____ you _____ we'll need?
5 We _____ our regular team meeting on Thursday morning.

8 **Put the sentences into the correct order to make two conversations about arranging meetings. The first line is done for you in each one.**

Conversation 1
a No problem. What date do you have in mind? ___
b OK. I look forward to meeting you on the 3rd at ten. ___
c Fine. The 1st, 2nd and 3rd are all OK for me. ___
d Could we schedule a meeting sometime next month? _1_
e Let's go for Wednesday the 3rd then, at ten o'clock. ___
f How about the beginning of the month? ___

Conversation 2
a The 10th at nine o'clock…that's fine. ___
b Sure, I was thinking about the 10th or 11th of April. ___
c I'm free on both of those dates. ___
d Yes, would you like to suggest a date? ___
e Could we find a time to meet? _1_
f OK, let's settle for Tuesday the 10th then at, say, nine? ___

9 **Complete the next two conversations with words or phrases from the box.**

for me   get back   o'clock   next week   Tuesday 9th   business trip

- Is there any chance of meeting ¹_____ ?
- Sorry, I can't make next week. I'm away on a ²_____ .
- OK. Let's meet after you ³_____ .
- Yes, sure, how about Monday 8th or ⁴_____ ?
- I'm happy with the 8th. At 11 ⁵_____ ?
- 11 is great ⁶_____ .

16.00 GMT   problem   I'll try   in mind   board members   of the 15th

- Can you organize a conference call for all the ⁷_____ ?
- Sure. What date do you have ⁸_____ ?
- I was thinking ⁹_____ .
- That might be a bit too short notice, but ¹⁰_____ .
- Great. Can you schedule the call for ¹¹_____ ?
- No ¹²_____ .

For more on times and dates, see Units 3, 4 and 5.

Over to you

10 **Prepare answers to these questions.**
   1 How often do you make phone calls in English to organize meetings?
   2 Do you prefer to try to arrange meetings by email? Why? / Why not?

11 **Now interview other colleagues about arranging meetings. Make a note of their answers and report back your findings.**
   - How often?
   - What type of meetings?
   - By email or telephone?

I interviewed five people. Most of them make a phone call in English to organize a meeting about once a month. The most common type of meeting is…

12 **Imagine that an English client is phoning you to arrange a meeting. Fill in the gaps with replies so that the conversation makes sense.**

   Can we arrange to meet sometime?
   _____

   I'm tied up at the end of the week. What about next Monday?
   _____

   I'd prefer Monday morning actually.
   _____

13 **5 Now listen to a model answer. Try to write it exactly as you hear it. Then check your answer with the listening script on page 99.**

   Can we arrange to meet sometime?
   _____

   I'm tied up at the end of the week. What about next Monday?
   _____

   I'd prefer Monday morning actually.
   _____

14 Now turn to Case study 2 on page 86 for practice on arranging to meet.

15 For a list of expressions from this unit, see Useful language Unit 2 on page 94.

Unit 3 Writing emails in preparation for meetings

Background

Once a meeting is arranged, most follow-up correspondence is usually done by email – which involves a whole new set of language and conventions. Let's take a look at how they deal with this at Delta International.

Culture point – 'Chatty emails' In some cultures it is normal to write very friendly emails even in a business context. People often write as if they were chatting to somebody and they don't always check their spelling or grammar. What is it like in your country? Do people treat emails formally or informally?

Skills work

1   Read the following four emails (A–D) and write the correct letter(s) next to the explanatory sentences (1–7).

Which email(s)…
1   is a request for a list of completed aims? _____
2   is about a meeting for company shareholders? _____
3   is about a meeting for sharing ideas? _____
4   are about staff development? _____
5   is sent to more than one person? _____
6   have an attachment? _____
7   mentions booking accommodation? _____

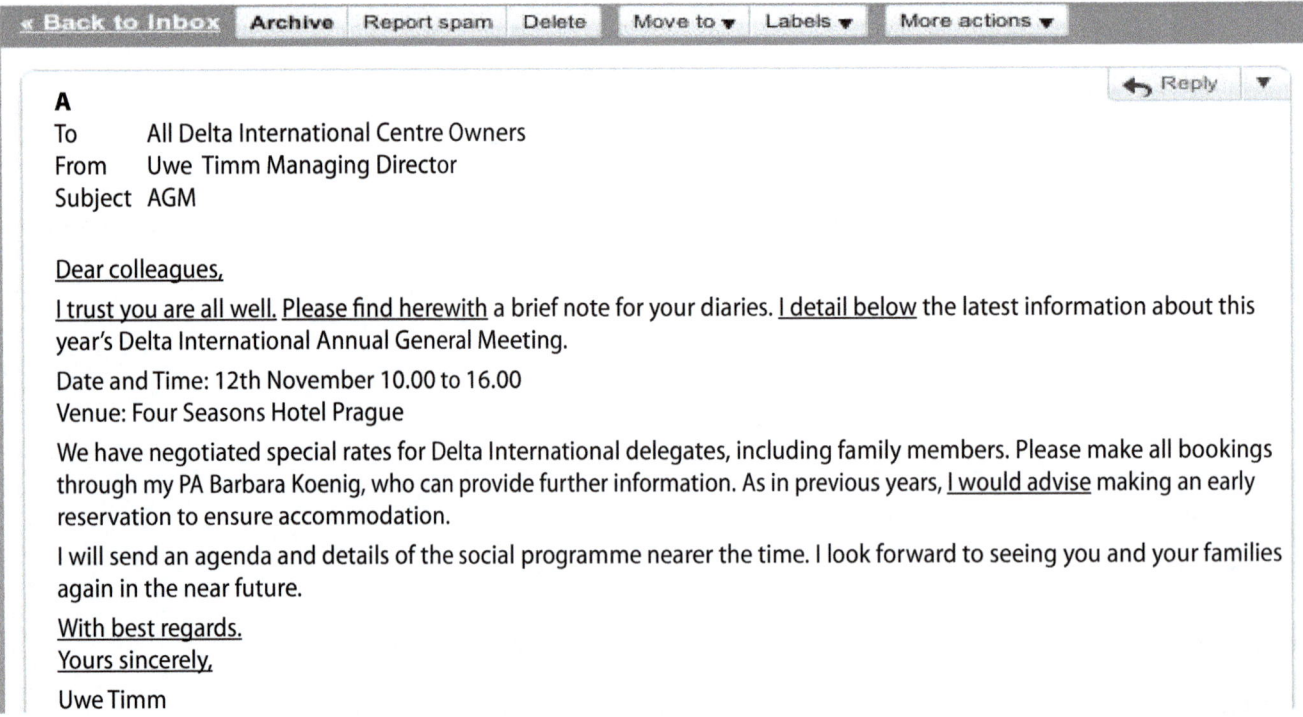

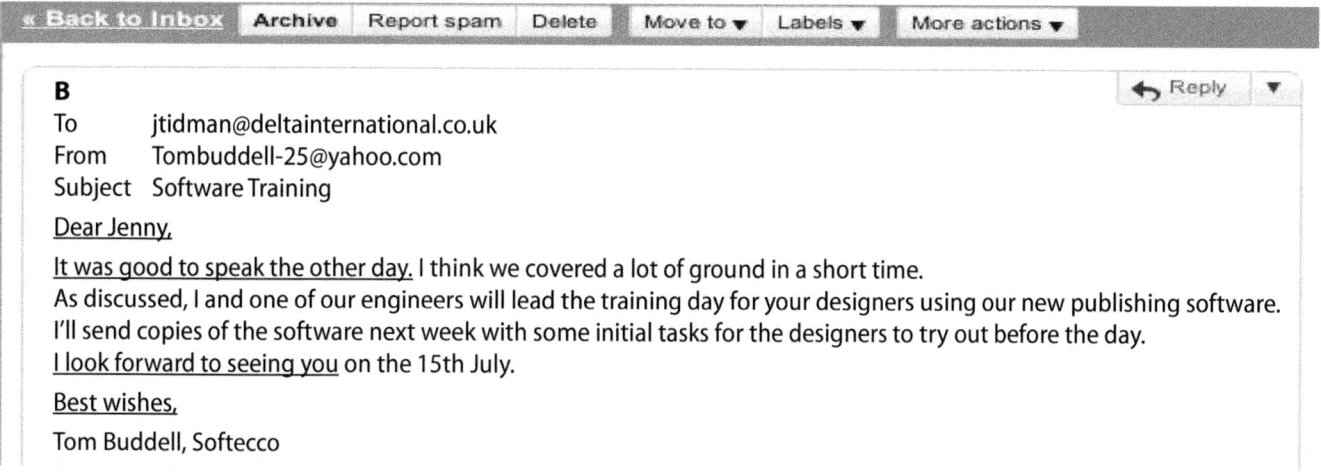

B

To jtidman@deltainternational.co.uk
From Tombuddell-25@yahoo.com
Subject Software Training

Dear Jenny,

It was good to speak the other day. I think we covered a lot of ground in a short time.

As discussed, I and one of our engineers will lead the training day for your designers using our new publishing software. I'll send copies of the software next week with some initial tasks for the designers to try out before the day.

I look forward to seeing you on the 15th July.

Best wishes,

Tom Buddell, Softecco

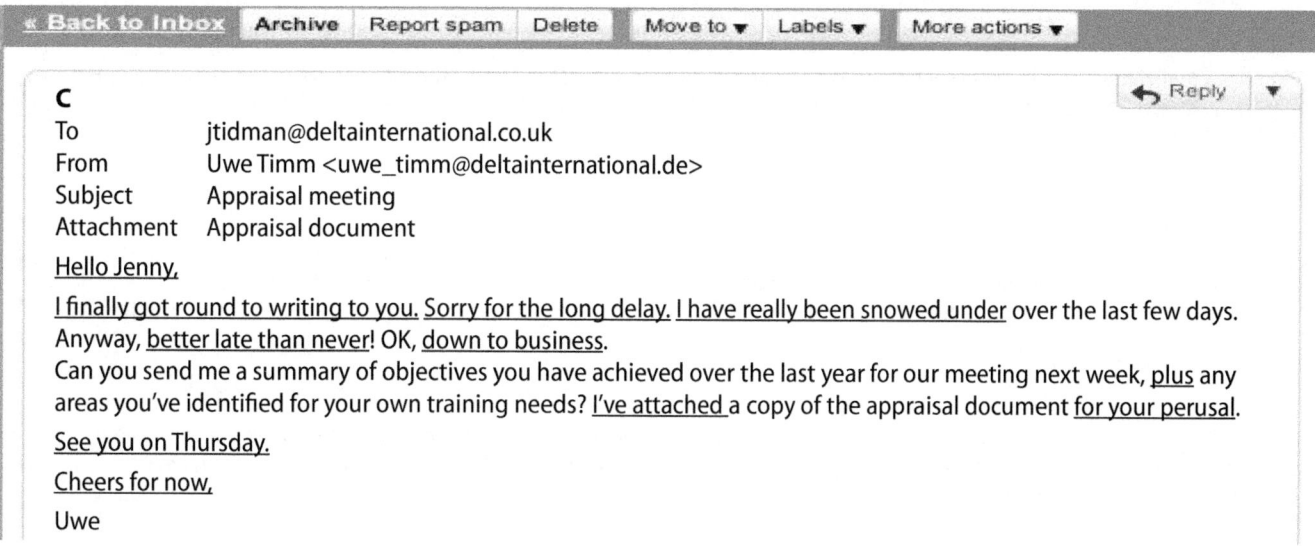

C

To jtidman@deltainternational.co.uk
From Uwe Timm <uwe_timm@deltainternational.de>
Subject Appraisal meeting
Attachment Appraisal document

Hello Jenny,

I finally got round to writing to you. Sorry for the long delay. I have really been snowed under over the last few days. Anyway, better late than never! OK, down to business.

Can you send me a summary of objectives you have achieved over the last year for our meeting next week, plus any areas you've identified for your own training needs? I've attached a copy of the appraisal document for your perusal.

See you on Thursday.

Cheers for now,

Uwe

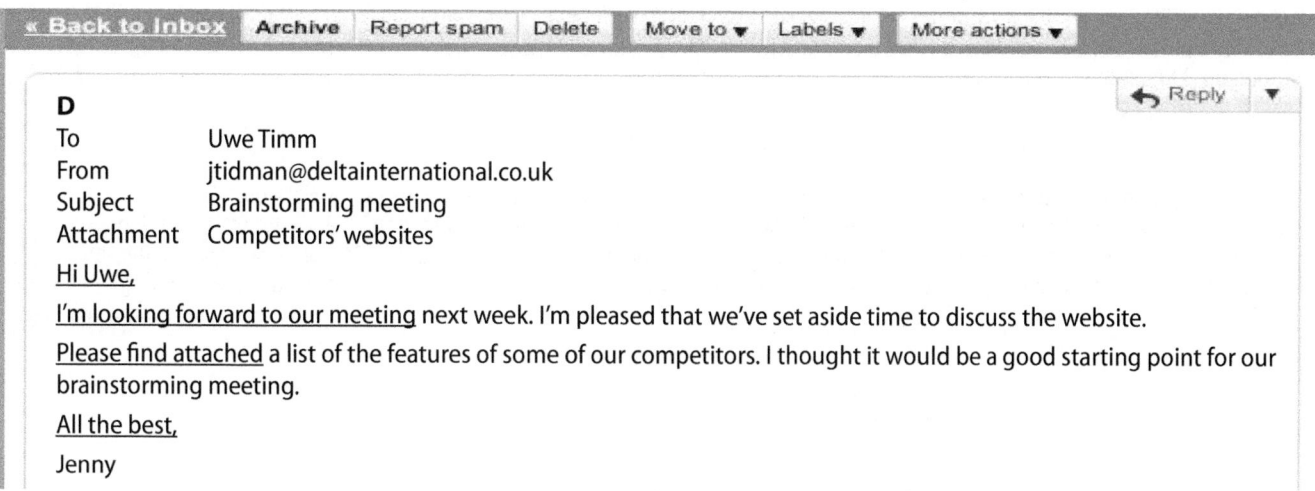

D

To Uwe Timm
From jtidman@deltainternational.co.uk
Subject Brainstorming meeting
Attachment Competitors' websites

Hi Uwe,

I'm looking forward to our meeting next week. I'm pleased that we've set aside time to discuss the website.

Please find attached a list of the features of some of our competitors. I thought it would be a good starting point for our brainstorming meeting.

All the best,

Jenny

2   Read the emails again and decide which is the most formal and the most informal.

3 Now complete the table with the underlined words and phrases from the emails in 1.

Formal	Informal

4 Read these people's ideas about writing emails. Then complete sentences 1–6 below with the first name of the correct person.

I think it's really important to write a short but very clear message in the subject line. That way the reader gets the key point of your message the moment he opens the mail. It also means that the reader can quickly find the mail again if necessary. Some people leave the subject line blank. That's not very professional in my opinion.
Tony Davey

In my opinion the most important thing is to be as brief as possible. It's good as well if the reader can reply with just yes or no answers. So I never write questions like: 'Can you give me an idea of what you think about possible dates?' I always write short questions like: 'How about Friday at 9am for the meeting?'
Jeremy Rooster

For me the most important thing is to make the text easy to read. I use headings and a very clear font. I also underline key words or phrases. It's important as well to use paragraphs to separate key points. I also think that it's better and clearer if an email only deals with one main point.
Olga Birch

I like to make my emails fun – even the business ones. I write in a chatty way as if I were speaking to the person. I also use lots of symbols to liven things up a bit. For example: 'That was a great idea! 😊😊' I sometimes write key words in capital letters, but I know that annoys some people.
Salina Crouch

I think a lot of people send emails without checking them first. This can lead to problems and some very embarrassing situations. I always proofread what I've written and always have one last look before I press the 'send' button. I also think that it's important not to send an email if the message is very private, because it's easy for the person receiving it to forward it to somebody else by mistake. Also, if you forward an email I think it's essential to give a reason why you're forwarding.
Marmen Hofmeister

1 _____ likes emails to be like informal conversations.
2 _____ likes to write very short emails.
3 _____ likes to use lots of emoticons in emails to liven them up.
4 _____ likes to have a very clear layout that is easy to read quickly.
5 _____ likes to make sure that the subject of the email jumps off the page.
6 _____ likes to read through emails very carefully to check for mistakes before sending them.

For more on opinions, see Unit 12.

5   Now write your views about emails, using the comments in 4 as a model.

In my opinion,

Further practice

6   **6** Pronunciation practice. Listen to the email addresses and repeat them.

jtidman@deltainternational.co.uk
Tombuddell-25@yahoo.com
uwe_timm@deltainternational.de

7   Now ask three other people you know for their email address and write them down.

> **Key words**
> **correspondence** (noun): the process of writing and receiving letters or emails
> **look forward to** (phrase): to feel happy about something that is going to happen
> **negotiate** (verb): to try to reach an agreement by discussing something in a formal way
> **request** (noun): the act of asking in a polite or formal way

8   Present continuous. Make full sentences in the present continuous. The first one done for you.
   1   I / look forward / meet you next week   *I am looking forward to meeting you next week.*
   2   Our biggest client / visit / today
   3   the printer / work?
   4   He / not sit / his office
   5   you / come / the meeting?

Over to you

9   Prepare answers to these questions.
   1   How often do you write emails to participants after you have arranged a meeting?
   2   Who do you write to? (Customers, clients, suppliers, English-speaking colleagues?)
   3   What type of emails do you write in English? (Long, short, formal, informal?)

10 Now interview other colleagues about the emails they write. Make a note of their answers and report back your findings.

11 Read email B from exercise 1 again. Imagine you are Tom Buddell from Softecco. Instead of sending an email, you have to telephone Jenny Tidman and leave a message on her answer phone about the training day. Write out your message, then practise saying it.

12 Now turn to Case study 3 on page 87 for more practice on writing emails.

13 For a list of expressions from this unit, see Useful language Unit 3 on page 94.

Unit 4 Confirming and rescheduling meetings

Background

In the previous unit we looked at how emails can be used to plan meetings. Of course, emails, verbal communication or a combination of the two can also be used to change arrangements – which is what we find the Delta International staff trying to do in this unit.

> *Culture point – 'Losing face'* Some people don't like disappointing others. They may, therefore, find it difficult to cancel or postpone a scheduled meeting – perhaps even preferring not to go to the meeting rather than informing you that they can't attend! Do you know anyone like this? How much do you think this varies by culture?

Skills work

1. Read the endings of some conversations between Delta International staff. Fill in the gaps with the words and phrases from the box.

   | decided   note   go over   check   forward   back   see   forget   after   confirm   right |

UWE: So can I just ¹_____ those details with you again? Your team meeting is on Thursday morning from 9.30 to 10.30, and I could join you at 10.15 for the last fifteen minutes?
PAUL: Yes, that's ²_____ . 10.15 would be great.

JENNY: Let me just make a ³_____ of that before I ⁴_____ . Tuesday afternoon at two o'clock.
PAUL: Yes, and you're coming to us in the design office.
JENNY: Sure.

JENNY: OK, so ⁵_____ you on Wednesday at four o'clock. In your office?
UWE: No, I think it's best if we use the small seminar room.

UWE: OK, so we've ⁶_____ on the 12th of November then?
RICK: Yes, can you send a mail to the board members to ⁷_____ that?
UWE: Sure, I'll mail everybody ⁸_____ our call.

PAUL: So to ⁹_____ : you'll suggest the 15th to the training company and get ¹⁰_____ to me to confirm?
JENNY: Sure, I think the 15th will be OK though.
PAUL: I'm looking ¹¹_____ to the session. I've heard the trainer is very good.

2 **Listen to the recording to check your answers to 1.**

3 **Make sentences to confirm arrangements. Draw lines to connect the phrases in each column. The first one is done for you.**

1 Can I check	forward	meeting with	you again?
2 Let me make	you on Wednesday	date and the time before	at 10 o'clock.
3 So I'll see	a note of the	to seeing you on the 5th	I forget.
4 Let	the details of the	go	over that again.
5 I'm looking	me just	at four o'clock in your office,	OK?

For more on confirming action and deadlines, see Unit 17.

4 **Put this conversation between Uwe Timm and Paul Hoffman into the correct order. The first line is done for you.**

a Something has come up and I can't get out of it. ___
b Hello Paul. Uwe here. _1_
c Paul, I'm terribly sorry, but I'm afraid I'm going to have to ask you if we can reschedule my meeting with you and the design team on Thursday. ___
d Brilliant! Sorry about this. It really couldn't be helped. ___
e Oh hi, Uwe. ___
f Oh, why's that? What's the problem? ___
g Is there any chance of postponing the meeting until the following week? Could we go for the same day and the same time? ___
h That's no problem. It's all right. Have you got another date in mind? ___
i Yes, that would be fine. ___

5 **Read emails A and B and then answer these questions.**
1 Why can't the engineer lead the training course?
2 Who is going to change the Delta International website?

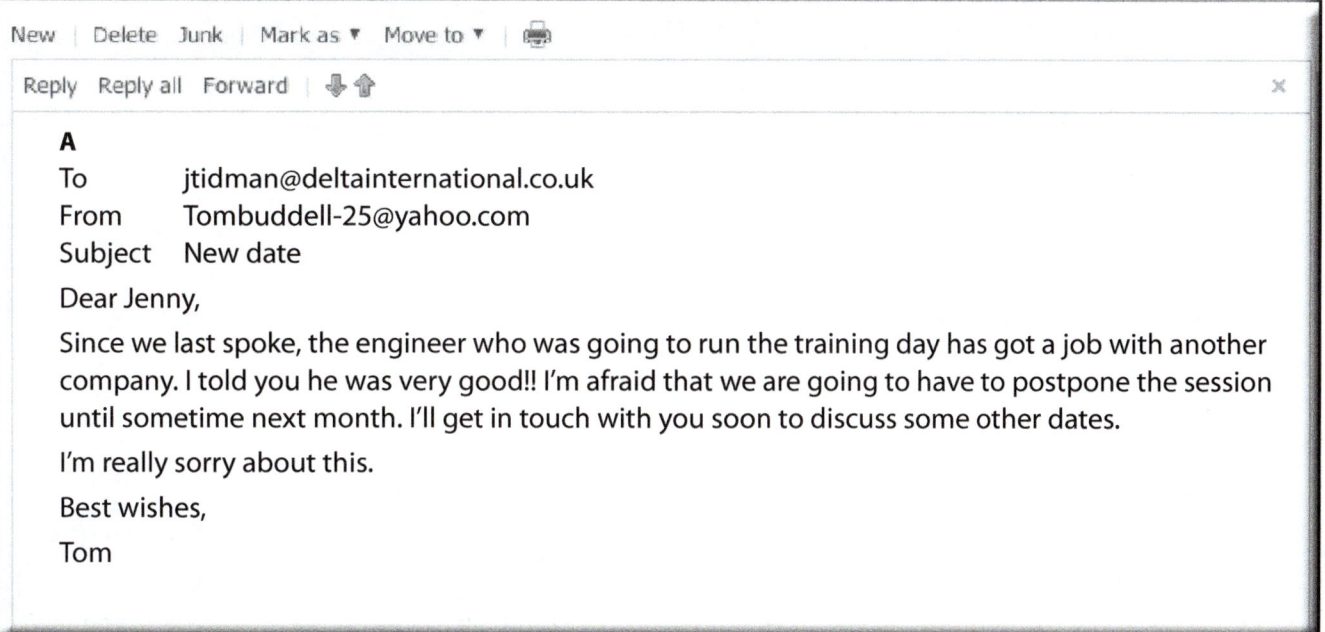

Unit 4 Confirming and rescheduling meetings

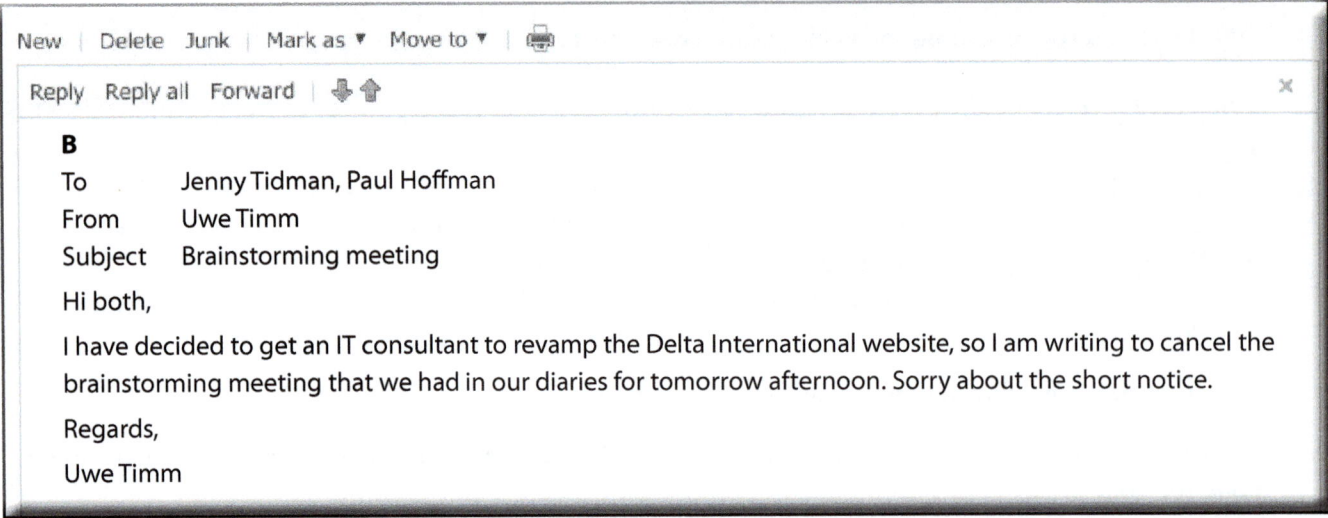

6 Read the emails again and then complete the gaps in the dictionary entries below with the correct verb: 'cancel' or 'postpone'.

> 1 _____: to decide not to have a meeting and to inform people of your decision
> 2 _____: to hold a meeting at a later date or time than originally scheduled

Further practice

7 *7* Pronunciation practice. Listen again to the conversations in 1 and repeat the lines. Then read the conversations aloud with a partner.

> **Key words**
> **confirm** (verb): to say something is definitely true
> **diary** (noun): a book with pages for each day where you can write things that you have to do
> **notice** (noun): information or a warning about something that is going to happen
> **revamp** (verb): to improve something by making major changes

8 Phrasal verbs. Match the phrasal verbs with the definitions.

1 go over   a to check carefully
2 get back to   b to contact
3 come up   c to avoid doing
4 get out of   d (eg a problem) to happen and need to be dealt with
5 get in touch with e to contact again at a later time

Over to you

9 Prepare answers to these questions.
  1 Are many of the meetings you are invited to cancelled or postponed?
  2 Have you ever been to a meeting and only found out when you arrived that the meeting had been cancelled/postponed?

10 Now interview other colleagues about their experience of cancelled or postponed meetings. Make a note of their answers and report back your findings.

11 Brainstorm with a partner the most common reasons for cancelling or postponing meetings. Then complete the mind map with your ideas.

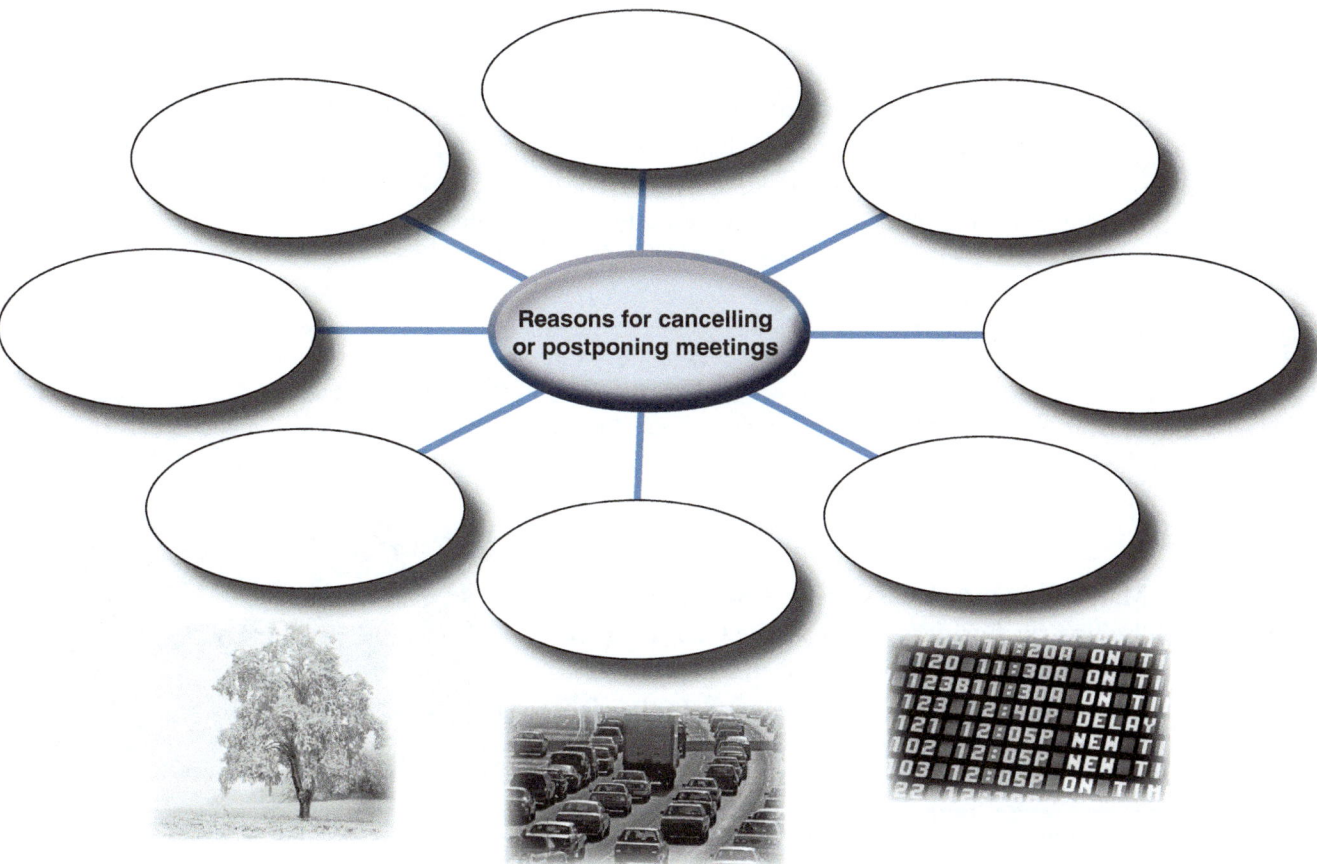

12 Read these possible reasons for cancelling a meeting. For each one, add a tick (✓) in the relevant column to show whether you agree or disagree that it is a suitable reason.

		Agree	Disagree
1	The meeting is too expensive and the outcome is too small.		
2	Decisions about the agenda can be made without consulting people.		
3	All issues can be dealt with by phone or email.		
4	The chairperson wants the afternoon off to play a round of golf.		
5	Everyone is busy and a meeting would disrupt work.		
6	The meeting is only to pass on information and not to make decisions.		
7	The issues are very controversial and would result in harmful conflict.		
8	It is a last-minute meeting and none of the paperwork has been circulated.		
9	The chairperson's PA, who takes the minutes, is in a bad mood.		
10	Some of the key decision-makers can't attend.		

13 Now turn to Case study 4 on page 87 for more practice on postponing and cancelling meetings.

14 For a list of expressions from this unit, see Useful language Unit 4 on page 94.

Unit 4 Confirming and rescheduling meetings

Unit 5 Booking a business centre for a meeting

Background

ArrowInsurance is an international insurance company which has offices in London, Qatar and Abu Dhabi. ArrowInsurance believes strongly in the value of providing its staff with regular skills training in leadership and management, marketing and sales. It organizes its courses mainly 'in house' and occasionally also in conference or business centres.

Culture point – Where to meet? Many companies now book meeting venues outside the company headquarters and sometimes even abroad. Can you think of the advantages and disadvantages of doing this? What problems might occur? What is it like in your country? Where does your company organize meetings?

Skills work

1   Emily Maitland is one of the staff at ArrowInsurance. She is telephoning the business centre at the Century Hotel in Doha, Qatar. Listen to the first part of the conversation, in which she asks about meeting rooms. Complete the right column of the table with the correct information.

1 Type of meeting:	
2 Date of the meeting:	
3 Number of delegates:	
4 Maximum number of people in the rooms: (Circle the correct number for each room)	• Room 1 48 84 • Room 2 36 30 • Room 3 60 16 • Room 4 8 18

2   Listen again and fill in the gaps with words from the box.

> available need mind booking provisional availability looking delegates split

1   I'm ringing about _____ the centre for a meeting.
2   Can I first check your _____ ?
3   What date did you have in _____ ?
4   We are _____ at June 13th.
5   Would you _____ the whole centre or just a selection of rooms?
6   We would need a room for thirty _____ at the start and end of the day.
7   We would like to _____ them into four or five groups for the rest of the time.
8   Another company has made a _____ booking for our presentation theatre that day.
9   All of the other rooms are _____ .

3   **9** Listen to the second part of the conversation and tick the facilities which are mentioned.

multimedia projector   photocopier   interactive whiteboard
fax machine   drinks machine   wireless Internet
television   video   DVD
laptop   newspapers and magazines car park
toilets   restaurant   reception area

For more on checking equipment, see Unit 11.

4   Choose the correct option in each sentence.
   1 Can you go <u>through</u> / <u>down</u> what you could offer us?
   2 Our biggest seminar room <u>holds</u> / <u>offers</u> 48 people.
   3 The <u>ground</u> / <u>floor</u> plan is on our website.
   4 Can you tell me about the <u>premises</u> / <u>facilities</u> in each room?
   5 We have <u>maintained</u> / <u>equipped</u> all our rooms to the highest standards.
   6 They have all you would expect from a <u>professional</u> / <u>expert</u> training centre.
   7 We can <u>serve</u> / <u>cater</u> refreshments in the training rooms or in our restaurant.
   8 The restaurant <u>seats</u> / <u>places</u> 50 delegates.

5   **8 9** Now listen to the full conversation again and check your answers to 4.

6   **10** Listen to Emily negotiating a price for the use of the business centre. Does she accept the final offer made by the centre?

7   **10** Listen again. Complete the sentences with the missing words.
   1 I'd like to discuss _____ for using the centre.
   2 I think I gave you an _____ of our standard rates.
   3 I am working to quite a tight _____ .
   4 I think you'll find that our rates are very _____ .
   5 I would need to have a lower price in order to be able to make a _____ .
   6 What sort of budget are you _____ to?
   7 If you could reduce your standard rate by _____ it would be possible.
   8 That's a rather big _____ .
   9 We couldn't do such a large discount for a _____ booking.
   10 If you could offer us some more business, he would make an _____ to our normal policy.
   11 I'd need to check with my _____ again.
   12 I'd like to take you _____ on that.

Further practice

8   **10** Pronunciation practice. Listen again to Emily's last conversation with the Century Business Centre and practise reading it aloud. Then work with a partner and prepare a similar dialogue. Make sure you change the names, discount and budget. You can also reject the offer if you want to.

> **Key words**
> **discount** (noun): a reduction in the price of something
> **facilities** (noun): equipment provided at a place for people to use
> **headquarters** (noun): the place where a company or organization has its main offices
> **venue** (noun): the place where an activity or event happens

9   Modal verbs. Fill in the gaps with a modal verb from the box. Use the information in brackets to help you.

| can | should | must | could | need |

1   I would _____ to check with my manager. (*necessity*)
2   You _____ return the keys by 4pm the following day. (*obligation*)
3   It is something we _____ sort out by email. (*ability*)
4   _____ you let me know as soon as possible? (*polite request*)
5   I _____ be able to give you an answer by the end of next week. (*probability*)

Over to you

10 Match the questions and answers.

1   Do you have availability on the 6th of June?
2   What dates do you have in mind?
3   Do you want to book the whole centre?
4   Have you got a room big enough for 30 delegates?
5   Can I make a provisional booking for the 6th of May?

a   No, only a selection of rooms.
b   Yes, we've got several seminar rooms for large groups.
c   No, we are fully booked on that date.
d   Yes certainly, but please confirm by the end of the month.
e   We were thinking of the 13th or 14th of March.

11 Prepare answers to these questions.
1   Do you ever book meeting rooms at a hotel or business centre? Or do you have a PA to do it for you?
2   What do you think are the five most important facilities for a meeting room?

12 Now interview other colleagues about booking meetings. Make a note of their answers and report back your findings.

13 Discuss with a partner where you normally meet people. Have you had meetings in the following places?
- in a hotel meeting room
- in a hotel reception
- in your office
- in a special meeting room at your office
- in a restaurant
- in a café/pub
- in a business centre

What is the most unusual place you have ever held a meeting in?

Are there any places that you think are definitely NOT appropriate for meetings? Why? Discuss with a partner and justify your point of view with reasons.

For more on opinions, see Unit 12.

14 You want to book a meeting room at a business centre. Look at the conversation below and give your own answers for the lines in italics. You can look at listening scripts 8, 9 and 10 on pages 99 and 100 for language.

> CLP Business Centre, Monica Bromma speaking. How can I help?
> *Say who you are and why you are ringing.*

> Yes, certainly.
> *Say that you would like to check their availability first.*

> Yes, of course. What date did you have in mind?
> *Give a date.*

> Would you need the whole centre?
> *Say how many delegates there will be and what rooms you will need.*

> That's no problem. Would you like to make a booking now?
> *Ask how much it will cost.*

> The total cost would be approximately 3000 Euros.
> *Say you are on a tight budget and ask if they would consider a discount.*

> What sort of budget are you working to?
> *Suggest a discount.*

> That could be possible, but unfortunately not for a one-off booking.
> *Suggest some other meetings that your company could hold at the centre.*

> In that case, I think we can give you the discount. Would you like me to send confirmation by email?
> *Say yes and give her your email address.*

> OK, I'll be in touch shortly with all the details. Thanks for your call.
> *Thank her and say goodbye.*

15 Now turn to Case study 5 on page 88 for more practice on booking a business centre.

16 For a list of expressions from this unit, see Useful language Unit 5 on pages 94 and 95.

Unit 5 Booking a business centre for a meeting

Unit 6 Planning meetings

Background

In the previous unit we saw Emily Maitland from ArrowInsurance negotiating a deal with the Century Business Centre in Doha. The booking went through successfully so we now find ourselves back in Doha for the ArrowInsurance training course.

> **Culture point – 'Dotting the 'i's'** In some cultures it is normal practice to plan everything in great detail and not leave anything to chance. In others people are happy with just an outline plan of action and prefer to work freely within that framework, responding flexibly to changing circumstances. What is it like where you are? And what sort of planner are you?

Skills work

1 Charles Toplitz is a consultant who regularly runs training courses for ArrowInsurance. Read his introduction to a session on planning meetings, and fill in the gaps with words from the box. Each word may only be used once.

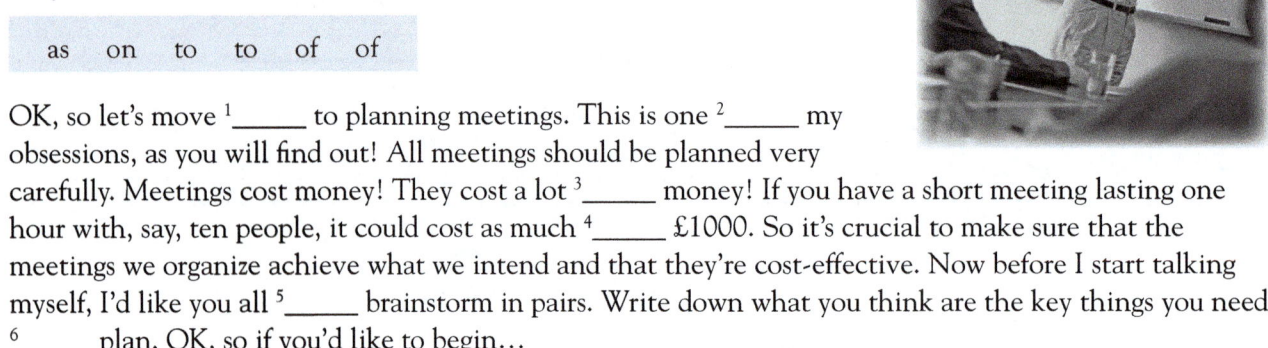

| as | on | to | to | of | of |

OK, so let's move ¹_____ to planning meetings. This is one ²_____ my obsessions, as you will find out! All meetings should be planned very carefully. Meetings cost money! They cost a lot ³_____ money! If you have a short meeting lasting one hour with, say, ten people, it could cost as much ⁴_____ £1000. So it's crucial to make sure that the meetings we organize achieve what we intend and that they're cost-effective. Now before I start talking myself, I'd like you all ⁵_____ brainstorm in pairs. Write down what you think are the key things you need ⁶_____ plan. OK, so if you'd like to begin…

2 Look up any words you don't know in the text in 1.

3 🔊 Listen to the results of the brainstorming. How many of Charles' points on the interactive whiteboard below do the participants mention? Tick the ones you hear.

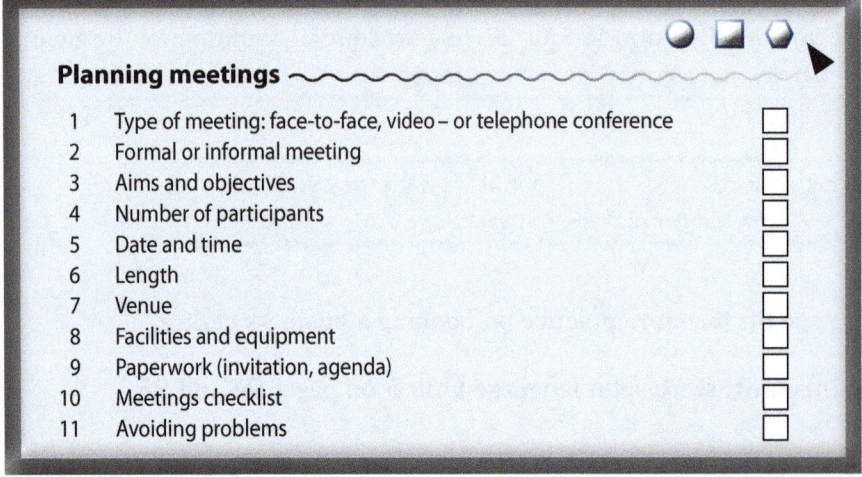

Planning meetings
1 Type of meeting: face-to-face, video – or telephone conference
2 Formal or informal meeting
3 Aims and objectives
4 Number of participants
5 Date and time
6 Length
7 Venue
8 Facilities and equipment
9 Paperwork (invitation, agenda)
10 Meetings checklist
11 Avoiding problems

4   **11** Look at the sentences below, which summarize some of the points made by the participants. Then listen again. Who made each point? Write the correct name next to each sentence.

Jerry    Sally    Sean    Paul

1   The equipment and facilities must match the needs of the meeting. _____
2   It's essential to be clear what type of meeting it is: formal or informal. _____
3   It's important to have a checklist of action points to help you plan. _____
4   It's vital that the venue for the meeting is appropriate. _____
5   It's crucial to decide if a face-to-face meeting is really needed, rather than a telephone or videoconference, for example. _____

5   **11** When making their points, the participants use five different adjectives meaning 'very important'. Listen again to the conversation and write down the five words. You can also look at the listening script on page 100 afterwards if you need to.

1   _____
2   _____
3   _____
4   _____
5   _____

6   Who do you think made the best point? Give at least one reason for your answer.

_____
_____
_____

7   Can you add any points of your own about planning meetings?

_____
_____
_____

8   Match the pairs to make positive comments and sentences to get participants involved.

1   Can we start   a   have a checklist of points.
2   So who'd like   b   some very good points.
3   Can we bring   c   to go next?
4   It's important to   d   really interesting.
5   That's   e   you in now, Paul?
6   You've made   f   with you?

For more on bringing people into the conversation, see Units 14 and 18.

Unit 6 Planning meetings

9   Read the ten extracts from Charles' talk. Which of the points are most important? Write a number (1–10) next to each one to arrange them in priority order, and give reasons for your choices.

- Morning meetings are more productive than meetings held at the end of the day.
- The chair must be absolutely clear about what he/she wants to achieve.
- The chair needs to know how many people will be at the meeting.
- There should be an agenda for nearly all meetings.
- The organizer must check that all the equipment needed is available and in good working order.
- The chair must ensure that all participants are informed of the meeting in good time.
- Refreshments must be available for longer meetings.
- The chair should stop people wasting time or not sticking to the agenda.
- The chair must decide if a meeting is necessary. It might be possible to achieve the objectives by email.
- The chair must ensure that the meeting runs smoothly.

Further practice

10   **12** Pronunciation practice. Listen to the following sentences, paying particular attention to the underlined words. Are the vowel sounds in these words weak or strong? Write the correct answer next to each sentence. The first two are done for you.

   1   We spoke about lots <u>of</u> simple, practical points. *Weak*
   2   Can we hear now what you've come up <u>with</u>? *Strong*
   3   We thought it was essential to be clear what type of meeting it <u>was</u>.
   4   That's <u>a</u> good comment.
   5   We thought about having a checklist <u>as</u> well.
   6   <u>And</u> linked to that, of course, is the question of equipment and facilities.

   Then repeat the sentences.

> **Key words**
> **cost-effective** (adjective): giving the most profit or advantage in exchange for the amount of money that is spent
> **paperwork** (noun): the documents you need for a particular activity
> **productive** (adjective): achieving good results

11 Phrasal verbs. Fill in the gaps with the correct form of the verbs from the box.

| come up with | stick to | draw up | sort out |

1   The new manager was very creative and _____ lots of new ideas.
2   The marketing department has _____ a sales strategy for us to consider in our team meeting.
3   I think it's very important that we _____ our objectives when things get difficult.
4   She was fantastic – she _____ the problem so quickly.

Over to you

12 Prepare answers to these questions.
   1   When was the last time you planned a meeting or another type of event? How did it go? What did you do? Was there anything you could have done better?
   2   What sort of problems might arise as a result of over-planning? Complete the mind map with your ideas.

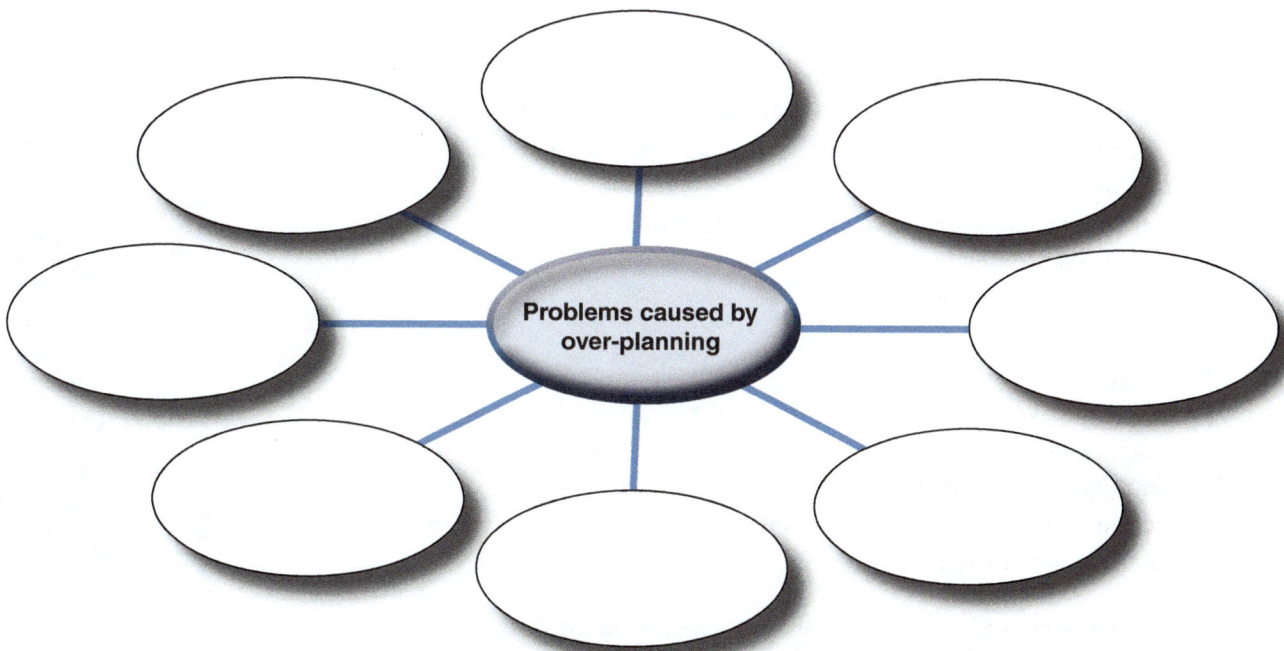

13 Now interview other colleagues about their experience of planning meetings or other events. Make a note of their answers and report back your findings.

14 Look again at the interactive whiteboard in exercise 3. Imagine you are Charles. Make a presentation about planning meetings to a group of colleagues. Use points from exercises 12 and 13 to guide you.

15 Now turn to Case study 6 on page 89 for more practice on planning meetings.

16 For a list of expressions from this unit, see Useful language Unit 6 on page 95.

Unit 6 Planning meetings

Unit 7 Networking before a meeting

Background

AquaTec, a Canadian company based in Toronto, has merged with a small company in Norway called Seamap, which produces satellite navigation systems for ships. This is the first time some of the senior managers and engineers from the two companies have met face-to-face.

Culture point – 'Breaking the ice' Before the start of most formal meetings, there is often an opportunity for participants to meet each other informally over coffee to 'break the ice' (make them feel less shy or nervous). It is important to make the most of this time, using 'small talk' (informal conversation about general topics) to network with as many people as possible. Can you think of a situation when you had to use small talk?

Skills work

1 **13** Listen to Vadim Gyduk, one of Seamap's managers, reporting to reception before the meeting. Tick the sentences that you hear.

   1 I'm here for the AquaTec/Seamap meeting.
   2 Let me just check your name off on the list.
   3 One moment, I'll ring and arrange for someone to meet you.
   4 You are in discussion group three.
   5 Here are the additional papers for the meeting.
   6 Here is your name badge.
   7 Take a seat over there, please.
   8 The meeting is on the fourth floor.
   9 Where can I leave my overcoat?
   10 You can leave your coat here in reception.
   11 And so where do I go now?
   12 Can I get you a cup of coffee?
   13 Coffee is being served in the Green Room.
   14 The lift is over there.

2 Practise a roleplay at reception with a partner. Student A is the visitor, student B the receptionist.

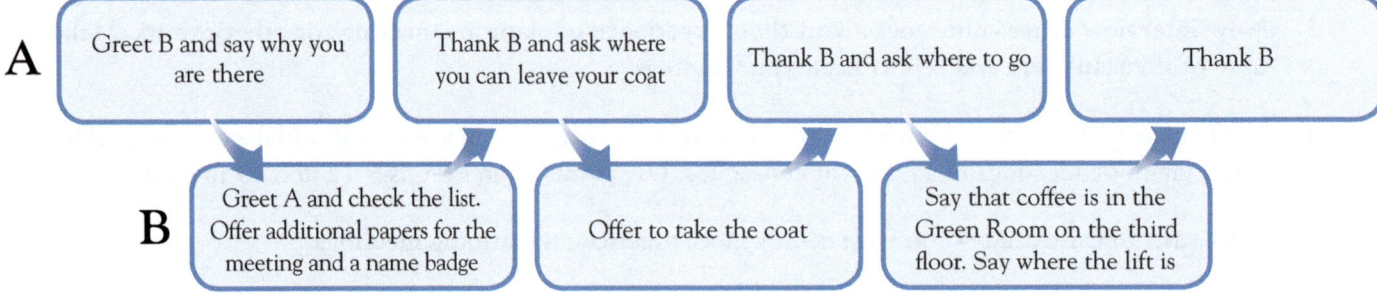

30   Unit 7 Networking before a meeting

3   Look at the pictures. Which six of the conversation topics given below do they represent? Write the correct picture number (1–6) next to six of the conversation topics.

refreshments   travel to the meeting   jobs   sport   physical appearance   salary

weather   accommodation   feelings   religion   family   politics

4   Which of the topics in 3 do you think are appropriate for small talk with strangers? Which topics are 'no-go areas' (not appropriate)?

5   With a partner, try to talk for 30 to 60 seconds about some of the appropriate small talk topics in 3.

6   **14** Listen to some small talk conversations. What is the main topic of each one? Write in the relevant topics from exercise 3 on the lines below.

   1 _____
   2 _____
   3 _____
   4 _____
   5 _____

Which conversation is not appropriate? Why?

7 Match the sentence halves to make small talk.

1 Nice to see you again!
2 Shall we have a chat over lunch?
3 How are you?
4 This is Hedda.
5 How was your flight?
6 Are you staying near here?
7 Can I get you another coffee?
8 What was the weather like when you left New York?

a Pleased to meet you.
b Very well thank you. And you?
c Yes please. That's very kind of you.
d Sure, great! Look forward to it.
e Great to see you too!
f Really hot! Much warmer than here!
g Yes, I'm booked in at the Hilton.
h Terrible! We were delayed three hours.

8 Put this small talk conversation into the correct order. The first line is done for you.

a Hi, pleased to meet you, Alina. I'm Jane Searby. ___
b So you had quite a long journey to get here? ___
c Hello, have we met before? _1_
d Well, my name's Alina Davey. I'm in the production team at AquaTec. ___
e Yes, but I got a direct flight so it wasn't too bad. ___
f No, I'm in sales. I'm one of the sales reps. I work mainly in South America. ___
g No, I don't think so. ___
h Nice to meet you, Jane. Are you in production as well? ___

Further practice

9 🔊 15 Pronunciation practice. Listen to the conversation in 8 and repeat the lines. Then practise reading the whole dialogue aloud with a partner.

10 🔊 16 Read the questions and write in your answers. Then listen to the original dialogue.

SVEN: Hi there. Long time no see!
YOU: _____
SVEN: So what are you up to now then?
YOU: _____
SVEN: Really! That's good news! Really good news. And how was your flight?
YOU: _____
SVEN: Oh, sorry to hear that. Did you get a taxi from the airport?
YOU: _____
SVEN: Are you staying near the conference centre then?
YOU: _____
SVEN: Can I get you another coffee, before we go into the meeting?
YOU: _____

> **Key words**
> **appropriate** (adjective): suitable or right for a particular situation or purpose
> **network** (verb): to meet and talk to people in order to receive or give information, especially about business opportunities
> **stranger** (noun): someone who you don't know

11 Make suggestions with either *shall* or *let's*. The first one is done for you.
1   meet for a drink *Let's meet for a drink.*
2   chat over lunch?
3   go and have a coffee
4   sit over there?
5   get a taxi back to the hotel

For more on making suggestions, see Unit 12.

Over to you

12 Prepare answers to these questions.
1   Do you find it easy to talk to people that you don't know? Why? / Why not?
2   What advice would you give to someone to improve their small talk skills?

13 Read these tips about small talk. Which do you think are the best tips? Share your ideas with a partner.

Small talk to the top!

Small talk can be difficult if you are not used to talking to people you don't know, but you can learn to be really good at it. Here are some tips to help you:

1. Try to talk in English to people who you meet in shops, in the lift and in cafés. Practise small talk by chatting to everybody!
2. Watch the news in English on TV or listen to the radio. It's always good to be able to talk about things that are in the news.
3. Always accept invitations to dinners with friends, office parties and other social occasions. They are perfect opportunities for small talk!
4. Good topics for small talk are television, music, sport and fashion. So prepare something interesting to say on one or two of these topics.
5. Keep a note of funny stories you've heard, nice or terrible places you've visited, unusual things you've seen or interesting people you've met.
6. Practise small talk by talking to yourself in the mirror.
7. Write topics on bits of paper, then pick them at random and see if you can talk about them for 30 seconds.
8. Try to do some new things. Go to a new restaurant, read a book by a new author, learn a new language or run a marathon. These could all be good topics for small talk!
9. Learn to be a good listener, so you can ask questions which show you are interested in the other person.

14 Write your own small talk conversation. Try to include at least three appropriate small talk topics. Then practise saying the conversation without looking at your notes.

15 Now turn to Case study 7 on page 89 for an interactive small talk activity.

16 For a list of expressions from this unit, see Useful language Unit 7 on page 95.

Unit 8 Opening a meeting

Background

After the small talk and networking, it is time for the AquaTec and Seamap representatives to start the meeting that they are all here for. But how do they get down to business? In this unit we will find out exactly how to open a meeting.

> **Culture point – Following instructions** It is not always easy to get all the participants into the meeting room after coffee, particularly if some of them have difficulty understanding polite requests. For example, 'I think it's time we made a start' really means 'Get moving and fast!'. Are you polite like this in your language or are you more direct?

Skills work

1   Look at how the president of AquaTec attracts people's attention at the beginning of the meeting, and fill in the gaps with words from the box.

   sorry   attention   discuss   colleagues   fun   time

   Dear ¹_____ ! ² _____ to interrupt your ³ _____ , but could I have your ⁴ _____ please? Well, first of all I'd like to introduce myself formally to everybody. I'm Bernie Goodman, the president of AquaTec. We have a pretty big agenda today. We have a lot to ⁵ _____ , so could I ask you to start making your way to the meeting room? I think it's ⁶ _____ we made a start. The meeting room is over there, by the way, on the right.

   What friendly, less formal phrase does the president use to get people's attention?

2   Find words or phrases in the text in 1 which mean:
   1   going _____
   2   enjoyment _____
   3   co-workers _____
   4   plan of the meeting _____
   5   to present _____
   6   to stop _____

3   **17** Bernie is now about to open the meeting. Listen and read what he says. What document does he mention and why is it so important?

   'I think we're all here. That was pretty quick, thanks. I think we can launch proceedings now, so let's get the ball rolling. A warm welcome to everybody. On behalf of the whole AquaTec team, I'd like to say how pleased I am to meet up with our colleagues from Seamap. So a really warm welcome to the staff from Seamap! We've drawn up an agenda for the meeting. Does everybody have a copy? Is there anybody who didn't get a copy, by any chance? No? OK, great. Our administration seems to be working at last! OK, no more feeble jokes then, let's get this show on the road!'

4 Write down three expressions from the text in 3 that Bernie uses to start the meeting. Are they formal (F) or informal (I)? Circle the correct alternative for each expression.

1 _____ F / I

2 _____ F / I

3 _____ F / I

Why do you think he uses some informal language?

5 Now read the first part of the agenda below. Fill in the gaps with words from the box.

| Venue | Participants | Date and time | Apologies | Objective | Agenda |

1 _____

2 _____ : Present the new company structure

3 _____ : A1 Conference Centre, Bergen

4 _____ : Tuesday 10 June, 10am – 4pm

5 _____ : Bernie Goodman (Chair), Alina Davey, Vadim Gyduk, George Masterman, Jane Searby, Mark Field, Volker Flo, Debbie Garner, Dan Bushnell, Sven Wihlborg, Peter Harris, Sally Wicks (PA)

6 _____ : Renate Bromma, Tony Adams

6 🔊18 Listen to how Bernie continues his introduction and answer the following questions.

1 Why isn't Renate Bromma at the meeting?
2 What role does Bernie's PA have in the meeting?
3 What sort of lunch are they having?
4 What are they doing immediately after the meeting?

7 🔊18 Listen again and tick the things that Bernie does.

1 He starts with formalities and some organizational matters.
2 He explains the items on the agenda.
3 He mentions that two people are absent from the meeting.
4 He introduces the finance director.
5 He introduces his personal assistant.
6 He says that his PA will take the minutes.
7 He says that lunch will be at one o'clock.
8 He points out that there will be a tour of the factory after the meeting.
9 He talks about transport to the hotel after the tour.
10 He invites everybody to dinner.

Unit 8 Opening a meeting

8   **18** Listen to Bernie again. Find phrases (a maximum of five words each time) which mean the same as the following. The first one is done for you. You can check the listening script on page 101 if you need to.
   1   write a record of what is discussed in the meeting   _____take the minutes_____
   2   very busy   _____
   3   has said she can't come to the meeting   _____
   4   we're intending   _____
   5   the way the day is organized   _____
   6   looking at everybody in the meeting   _____
   7   a small number of things to be done at the start of every meeting   _____

Further practice

9   Put the lines of the following meeting introduction into the correct order. The first line is done for you.
   a   The afternoon session will be broken up with another coffee break. ___
   b   Well, after those apologies I would first like to introduce my new PA, Regina Slater. ___
   c   Dinner is planned for seven o'clock in the hotel restaurant. ___
   d   We'll then have lunch in the Green Room. ___
   e   After the meeting we can show you around the offices. ___
   f   Laura Morris, who works in sales, also sends her apologies. ___
   g   She is going to take the minutes. ___
   h   OK, so let's start the meeting proper by looking at the agenda. ___
   i   We plan to finish the meeting at about five. ___
   j   He's unable to attend the meeting because he is ill. ___
   k   Then there will be a short break for coffee. ___
   l   Firstly Arne Ziegert, our production manager, sends his apologies. ___
   m   After eating, we'll start up again at 1.15. ___
   n   Well, let's begin with some organizational matters. _1_
   o   After coffee we'll work through till 12.30. ___
   p   The plan is that we're aiming to work from now till 10.30. ___
   q   She is taking her annual leave at the moment. ___

10   **19** Pronunciation practice. Listen to the following job titles and <u>underline</u> the syllable that is stressed (the first one is done for you). Then repeat the words.
   de<u>si</u>gner   president   administrator   director   PA

> **Key words**
> **absent** (adjective): not present
> **formalities** (noun): things that must be done as part of an official process
> **interrupt** (verb): to say something to stop someone when they are speaking
> **proceedings** (noun): an event or series of related events

11   Present perfect tense. Make full sentences using the present perfect. The first one is done for you.
   1   My PA / draw up / agenda   My PA has drawn up the agenda.
   2   The finance director / send / apologies
   3   Sally / not distribute / minutes
   4   We / open / new factory
   5   He / have / sporting accident

Over to you

12 Prepare answers to these questions and discuss them with a partner.
   1 Do you often have to chair meetings? If so, what type of meetings do you chair?
   2 What are the most difficult things a chairperson has to do at the start of a meeting?

13 Read the following instructions for an activity to start a meeting in which a lot of people don't know each other. Do you think the activity would work? Why / Why not?

> **Introduction exchange**
>
> 1. Divide the group into pairs.
> 2. Give pairs about three or four minutes to ask and answer questions to learn something about each other.
> 3. Then ask each participant to introduce his/her partner to the other participants.
>
> The aim of this introduction is to point out the partner's qualities and to highlight the positive contribution that he/she will make to the meeting. You could say for example:
>
> *'This is Ilia. He works in the St Petersburg branch of the company in the marketing department. He is a very good team member and has lots of creative ideas. He loves trying to find solutions to very difficult problems.'*

14 Work in pairs. Do the activity described in 13. Interview your partner, making notes on the notepad below. Then introduce him/her to the rest of the class.

15 Now turn to Case study 8 on page 90 for a roleplay on starting a meeting.

16 For a list of expressions from this unit, see Useful language Unit 8 on page 95.

For more on opening and closing meetings, see Units 17 and 18.

Unit 8 Opening a meeting

Unit 9 Introducing yourself at a meeting

Background

CF Audits is a Dubai-based company which organizes quality control for a number of large international hotel chains in the Middle East. Its part-time auditors (people who check the hotels) are people who have to stay in hotels while travelling for their jobs. Today it is holding an introductory meeting in the Dubai Crowne Plaza hotel for a group of new 'mystery hotel guests'.

Culture point – Brief introductions In many countries it is normal to start a meeting by 'going round the table' and giving participants the opportunity to introduce themselves. Each person has to summarize his/her experience and present job in an interesting way so that people will remember them. Do you do introductions like this in your country?

Skills work

1 Stella Dobson, the training manager of CF Audits, has just started the meeting. Complete her brief personal introduction below with the correct past simple form of the words from the box. Each word may only be used once.

| start | complete | move | be | go | join | work |

Well, my own background is a bit unusual. I ^{1}_____ born in Abu Dhabi but my parents ^{2}_____ to Switzerland when I was nine and that's where I ^{3}_____ my secondary school education. The family then moved to France, where I ^{4}_____ to university. My first job was as a trainee manager in a hotel in Paris. After my training, I ^{5}_____ in different roles in hotels in the same chain all over the world. That was great experience for my present job. About five years ago I ^{6}_____ CF Audits and ^{7}_____ my current job six months ago. Well, that's me in a nutshell. So now it's over to you!

2 **20 21 22** Listen to three of the other introductions. Who do you think has the most interesting job? Who sounds the most interesting person?

3 **20** Listen again to Murat and decide if the statements about him are  true or false.
   1 He went to school in China.
   2 He studied engineering at a technical university in St Petersburg.
   3 His first job was as a road engineer for the government.
   4 He worked on road building projects all over Georgia.
   5 He is now a design engineer for the new Dubai metro.
   6 He is working on the rail link between Dubai and the airport.
   7 He has a good salary in Dubai.

4 **Now listen again to Cam and select the correct answer to the questions.**
1 Where did she go to school and university?
   a Vietnam b Hong Kong
2 Where did she work in Hong Kong?
   a in a store b in a hotel
3 Where did she emigrate to?
   a the UK b Canada
4 What is her current job?
   a stewardess for an airline b office manager for an airline

5 **Finally, listen again to Andre and answer the questions about him.**
1 Where was he born?
2 Where did he go to university?
3 What languages does he speak?
4 What is his current job?

6 **Imagine that these words describe your background. Write sentences. The first one is done for you.**
1 first / job / engineer My *first job was as an engineer.*
2 born / New York / school / Washington
3 two years ago / get / job / manager / hotel / Hong Kong
4 after school / study / medicine / university / Liverpool
5 start / current job / last year
6 now / doctor / hospital / France

7 **Use these example questions and responses to ask and answer personal questions.**

> Where were you born?
> *I was born in (…Germany/Japan/France.)*

> Where did you go to school?
> *I went to school in (…Berlin/Tokyo/Paris.)*

> Where and what did you study?
> *I studied (…law in Berlin/engineering in Tokyo/economics in Paris.)*

> What was your first job?
> *My first job was as (…a trainee in a law firm/a trainee engineer/an auditor with an insurance company.)*

> What is your current job?
> *I'm (…a lawyer/an engineer/an accountant.)*

> When did you join your present company?
> *I started my current job (…a year ago/two years ago/five years ago.)*

Unit 9 Introducing yourself at a meeting

Further practice

8   **23 Pronunciation practice.** Listen to the past simple forms and repeat them. Then put the verbs into the correct column according to the sound of their '-ed' ending. One word is already in place.

worked   started   ~~joined~~   studied   wanted   accepted   offered   travelled   moved   introduced

/d/	/ɪd/	/t/
joined		

> **Key words**
> **background** (noun): the type of family or culture that somebody comes from
> **current** (adjective): happening or existing now
> **experience** (noun): knowledge or skill that you gain over time spent doing a job or activity
> **summarize** (verb): to provide a short account of the most important facts or features of something

9   When you talk about your background in a meeting, the most common tense you use is the past simple. Look at listening scripts 20–22 on page 101 and find all the regular and irregular past simple forms. Then complete the chart with the infinitive and 'I' past simple form of each of the verbs.

Regular verbs		Irregular verbs	
Infinitive	Past simple 'I'	Infinitive	Past simple 'I'
to study	I studied	to go	I went

10 Find and correct the 8 verb mistakes in this personal introduction. The first one is done for you.

Hello, my name's Mona. I ~~am~~ born 28 years ago in Dubai. I attend school and university there. Later, I leave the UAE and go to England. I work in London for two years. After that period abroad I return to Dubai and I now worked as a sales manager for a hotel. When I lived abroad I really miss my home country, so it's great to be back.

1   am → was   5
2   6
3   7
4   8

Over to you

11 Prepare answers to these questions and discuss them with a partner.
   1 How often do you have to introduce yourself to people? What do you say?
   2 How should you adapt your personal introduction for business situations? What aspects should you focus on?

12 Make notes about yourself. Include something about your education, your first job and what you are currently doing.

   _____
   _____
   _____
   _____
   _____
   _____
   _____

   When you have finished, ask yourself the question: 'Is my introduction interesting enough?' If not, what can you add or change to make it more interesting?

13 Work in small groups. Introduce yourselves to each other, without looking at your notes if possible. As you listen to the other introductions, make notes in the box below on what your colleagues say about themselves. Then write the notes out in full, and compare them to your colleagues' original texts.

My name's Bond. James Bond. My code is 007. I am licensed to kill and I am currently working for MI6 as a spy.

14 Now turn to Case study 9 on page 90 for more practice on personal introductions.

15 For a list of expressions from this unit, see Useful language Unit 9 on page 96.

For more on introductions and greetings, see Unit 7.

Unit 10 Moving through the agenda and summarizing the discussion

Background

Once the meeting has begun and the introductions are over, all eyes turn to the agenda. But how does the chairperson effectively move through and sum up the points under discussion? Let's watch Stella in action.

> *Culture point – Walking or jumping?* Meetings in most cultures generally have an agenda. In some cultures people like to 'walk' through the agenda item by item, with fixed timing for each topic. In others people prefer to be more spontaneous and 'jump' from one item to another and then back again. What is it like where you are?

Skills work

1 **24** Look at the agenda below and listen to Stella presenting it. Then decide if statements 1–6 are true or false.

> Item 1 Introductions
> Item 2 The hotel chains to be audited
> Item 3 The audit documents and method of working (Ian Benson, marketing manager)
> Item 4 Salary and expenses
> Item 5 Allocation of hotels to mystery guests
> AOB (any other business)
> Buffet lunch

1 This is the first meeting that CF Audits has organized for new 'mystery hotel guests'.
2 The main aim of the meeting is team building.
3 The company has contracts to audit five hotels in Dubai.
4 The item about salaries and expenses will be the longest part.
5 One of the aims of the meeting is to decide on the dates of the audits.
6 Stella is going to talk about a new development under AOB.

2 Fill in the gaps in sentences 1–10 with the words from the box.

> item start aim words under business then fifth fourthly AOB

1 I'd like to say just a few _____ about today's agenda.
2 The _____ of this meeting is to prepare you to do the audits effectively.
3 We've all introduced ourselves. That was _____ 1.
4 _____ item 2 I'd like to talk about the hotel chains we're going to audit.
5 _____ under item 3 we need to focus on how the audits are conducted.
6 _____ , I will clarify salary and expenses for you.
7 The _____ item on the agenda is to decide who does what and when.
8 Then under any other _____ I'd like to mention a new development.
9 Does anyone have anything else you'd like to discuss under _____ ?
10 Any questions about the agenda or anything else, before we make a _____ ?

24 Then listen again to Stella and check your answers.

3 **25** Listen to Stella working her way through the items. Answer the questions as you hear them. There is a short pause followed by a beep between the relevant texts for each question.

1 What information does the summary document contain?
2 Why is Ian Benson going to talk about item 3?
3 What expenses will CF Audits pay for?
4 How does CF Audits match auditors to hotels?
5 What does Stella talk about under AOB?

4 Look at sentences 1–10 below, which can be used to either open or close items. Write the letter O (open) or C (close) next to each phrase, depending on their use.

1 OK then, let me talk you through item 2. ____
2 Does anyone have any further questions at this point? ____
3 Can we move on? ____
4 My colleague is going to talk us through the next item. ____
5 I think that really ties up that topic very neatly. ____
6 That definitely thoroughly covers that item. ____
7 OK, so that brings us to the next item. ____
8 Let's take up one of the most important topics. ____
9 Well, I think that issue seems to be resolved. ____
10 I think we've cleared up all the key points at this stage. ____

25 Listen again and check your answers.

5 Now read Stella's summary of the session. Complete the sentences by unscrambling the letters in brackets to make words that fit in the spaces.

OK, let me just go ¹_____ (hotrugh) what we discussed in this session. I'll try to ²_____ (ezumsmair) everything for you. We've ³_____ (dovrcee) four main points. ⁴_____ (ifystlr), we spoke about the hotel chains we are contracted to audit and you had the opportunity to look in detail at the portfolio of clients. Secondly, we had some ⁵_____ (thgenyl) input from Ian Benson, the CF Audits marketing manager, on all the new audit documentation and procedures. Thirdly, we went through expenses and fees and ⁶_____ (lyainfl) I summarized the way we allocate hotels to auditors.

6   Look again at the agenda in exercise 1, and write your own summary of the meeting. Begin with one of the following phrases:

- *I'll just run through what we covered.*
- *OK, let's go over some of the main points again.*
- *I'll just summarize the discussion.*
- *I think it might help to summarize what we discussed.*

_____

_____

_____

_____

Further practice

7   **26** Pronunciation practice. Listen to the following sentences and repeat them. Try to sound as natural as possible.

Let's turn to the next item.
Can you take us through the next topic?
I think that ties up that topic.
So, any more questions at this point?
I'll just run through what we covered.
Let's go over some of the main points again.

> **Key words**
>
> **clarify** (verb): to explain something more clearly so that it is easier to understand
> **cover** (verb): to include and deal with a particular situation, subject, etc
> **expenses** (noun): money that you spend as part of your job that your employer later gives back to you
> **summary** (noun): a short account of something that gives only the most important information

8   Phrasal verbs. Fill in the gaps with the correct form of the verbs in the box.

| tie up   go through   take up   clear up |

1   The committee _____ all the outstanding problems in yesterday's meeting.
2   I'd like to _____ that point under AOB. Is that OK with everybody?
3   We must _____ the report very carefully to check that there are no mistakes.
4   There are still a few loose ends to _____ before we can sign the contract.

Over to you

9   Prepare answers to these questions and discuss them with a partner.
   1   At what point do you think a chairperson should end the discussion on one item and move on to the next?
   2   Why is it a good idea to summarize the points being discussed? What might happen without these summaries?

10 Imagine you are Stella Dobson. Open and close items 2–5, and AOB, on the agenda. Look at exercise 4 in this unit, and listening script 25 on page 102, for help and ideas.

11 Read what some experienced chairpersons say about summarizing the discussion in meetings. Who do you most agree with?

Maybe if it's an official meeting there's no need for a summary because there will be very detailed minutes, but there are many meetings that I go to where this is not the case. I always do a summary, for example, if the meeting is about negotiating prices or doing some sort of deal. There I think it's essential for everybody to be clear about what has been agreed or decided. It's also important to clarify planned actions and who is going to do what. I often volunteer to do a summary myself, even if I am not in the chair. Usually people don't object to that and they are often grateful to have things made crystal clear.

Ahmed Kumar

I am always surprised by the fact that people get different messages from meetings. I think people just hear different things, or they hear the same things but get different messages. Sometimes people who hold very different views come out of the same meeting thinking that what they heard supported their own points of view. Because of this I think it's essential to clarify everything and summarize the discussion before people leave.

Natalie Hollingsworth

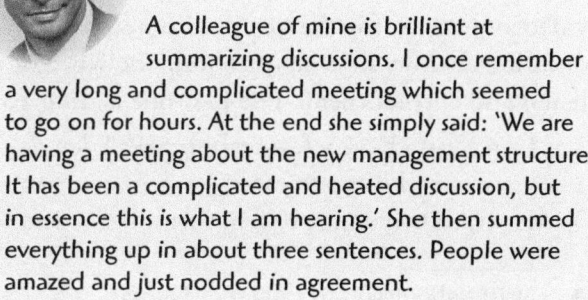

A colleague of mine is brilliant at summarizing discussions. I once remember a very long and complicated meeting which seemed to go on for hours. At the end she simply said: 'We are having a meeting about the new management structure. It has been a complicated and heated discussion, but in essence this is what I am hearing.' She then summed everything up in about three sentences. People were amazed and just nodded in agreement.

Martin Rodríguez

I remember one time. Just as we were about to close the meeting and leave, I asked if I could have the opportunity to summarize what I thought had been agreed. About halfway through my summary, as I was outlining a very important part of the deal, it became clear that it had not been resolved. We then had a lively discussion until the issue was sorted out. It was clear to everybody that if I had not volunteered to do the summary we would all have left the meeting without concluding everything.

Darina Howells

I think it's always better to do a written summary of a meeting even if there are no minutes taken. I usually summarize the main points in a follow-up email and ask people to come back to me to say whether or not they agree with them.

Seda Apaydin

12 For each of the people in 11, summarize their comments in a single sentence. The first one is done for you.

Natalie Hollingsworth: _A summary ensures that everyone comes away with the same message._
Ahmed Kumar: _____
Martin Rodríguez: _____
Darina Howells: _____
Seda Apaydin: _____

13 Now turn to Case study 10 on page 90 for more practice on talking about the agenda.

14 For a list of expressions from this unit, see Useful language Unit 10 on page 96.

Unit 11 Opening a videoconference

Background

Tara Products is an international company with its headquarters in Moscow. It produces skin and beauty care products, which it sells in over 20 countries worldwide through licensed distributors and a global network of Tara-branded beauty salons.

Culture point – Coping with technology First-hand experience of using IT varies greatly from country to country and company to company. Age can also be a factor: generally, the younger people are the more familiar they are with new technology. What is it like in your country? Have you had any training in videoconferencing, for example?

Skills work

1   **27** Listen to Natasha Ivanova, Tara's marketing director, opening a videoconference for the key distributors in Europe, and look at her questions below. In each question, one word or phrase is wrong – listen and correct them. The first one is done for you.

   1   Can I first check a few ~~technological~~ details? _technical_
   2   Can you all listen to me? _____
   3   Is anybody having problems with the sound or picture possibly? _____
   4   What about you in England, Nando? _____
   5   And what of Stefan in Berlin? _____
   6   How are things for you, Roger? _____
   7   Anything OK? _____
   8   Is that all better now, Carmen? _____
   9   Let's take a start, shall we? _____

2   **27** Listen again and match the people (1–4) to their experience of the equipment (a–d).

   1   Nando (Italy)   a   The sound and the picture are both bad.
   2   Stefan (Germany)   b   The sound isn't great but the picture is good.
   3   Roger (England)   c   The sound and picture are both good.
   4   Carmen (Spain)   d   The sound is perfect and the picture is OK.

3   Put an 'X' next to the sentences that don't make sense.

   1   The picture is very dark. I can see you perfectly.   ☐
   2   The sound is very distorted. I can't make out your voice.   ☐
   3   The sound is a bit crackly, but I can hear you well enough.   ☐
   4   There's no problem with the picture, but I can't see you at all.   ☐
   5   The picture quality is fine. I can see you clearly.   ☐
   6   The sound is crystal clear, but it's a bit crackly.   ☐

4 Make sentences about the sound and picture quality. Draw lines to connect the phrases in each column. The first one is done for you.

1 The sound is   you but   picture is dark.
2 The sound here   with the sound   the picture is clear.
3 There's no problem   bit crackly so   the sound is perfect.
4 The sound is a bit   delayed and the   and the picture is clear.
5 I can't see   OK and the picture   I miss every other word.
6 The sound is a   is a bit faint but   quality is fine as well.

> *Culture point – Setting the ground rules*
> In some cultures it is acceptable to talk at length, to interrupt others, to argue a point forcefully or to disrupt the planned schedule. It is sensible, therefore, for the chair of an international meeting to clarify 'ground rules' (the standard of behaviour you expect from all participants) at the beginning.

5 **28** Listen to how Natasha sets the ground rules for the discussion about the proposed new Tara logo and publicity campaign. Tick the things that she does in her introduction.

1 She welcomes everybody. ☐
2 She introduces herself. ☐
3 She mentions that some people are unhappy about the new company logo. ☐
4 She says that the aim of the meeting is to improve the proposed marketing campaign. ☐
5 She asks participants not to interrupt each other. ☐
6 She gives her opinion on the new logo. ☐
7 She asks people to make positive comments. ☐
8 She wants to make a short presentation and get the participants' reactions to it. ☐

6 Complete the ground rules using words from the box.

   alternative   positive   interrupt   one   hand   opinion

1 Firstly a very, very basic point – could I ask you all not to _____ when someone else is talking?
2 If you want to speak, can you raise a _____ ?
3 The rule is that we speak _____ at a time, so you all have the chance to put your views forward.
4 If we disagree about something, could we try and make our disagreement _____ ?
5 So instead of just saying that something is rubbish, can we suggest an _____ ?
6 I suggest that each person gives his or her _____ first and then we have a discussion round the table.

For more on introductions, see Unit 9.

Further practice

7 **29** Pronunciation practice. Now listen to the sentences in 6 and repeat them.

> **Key words**
> **crackly** (adjective): making continuous short sounds like wood burning
> **distributor** (noun): a company or person that supplies goods to shops
> **faint** (adjective): (eg sound) not strong or clear
> **raise a hand** (phrase): to put your arm in the air to show that you want to say something

Unit 11 Opening a videoconference

8 Tenses practice. Write the verbs in brackets in the correct tense.
   1 _____ your equipment _____ OK now? (work)
   2 I don't think we _____ _____ before. (meet)
   3 We _____ _____ a few problems with the picture at the moment. (have)
   4 I can't really hear you. The sound _____ still a bit faint. (be)
   5 We _____ _____ to an agreement last time. (not come)

9 The following lines are from a speech to set up ground rules in a meeting. Put the lines in the correct order. The first one is done for you.
   a Secondly, if you want to speak, can you please put up your hand? ___
   b And then, when you are speaking, please express your views positively. ___
   c So, don't just tell somebody that their ideas or opinions are rubbish. ___
   d Before we start, I'm going to make a few introductory comments about the ground rules. ___
   e OK then, I think that covers the ground rules. ___
   f I will then ask you to speak at an appropriate time. ___
   g Shall we start the meeting proper? ___
   h Firstly a very basic rule – could I ask you all not to interrupt when others are talking? ___
   i Welcome to the meeting, everybody. _1_
   j Similarly, if you disagree with somebody, can you also express your disagreement positively? ___

Over to you

10 Prepare answers to these questions and discuss them with a partner.
    1 In your opinion, what are the most important ground rules for a meeting?
    2 Do you think all of Natasha's ground rules are good? Why / Why not?

11 Here is another checklist of ground rules. How many of them were mentioned in your discussion of the questions in 10?

Tell participants that they should:
- arrive on time
- listen to each other
- only speak one at a time
- put up their hand if they want to speak
- not interrupt the person who is speaking
- use simple English
- not talk for too long
- talk slowly and clearly
- not speak with their hands over their mouths
- use words in full, for example 'business to business' rather than 'B2B'
- switch off their mobile phones.

12 Now work with a partner and write up your own preferred ground rules on the presentation screen below. Then use the screen to present the ground rules to the class, as if you were trying to set them up in a meeting.

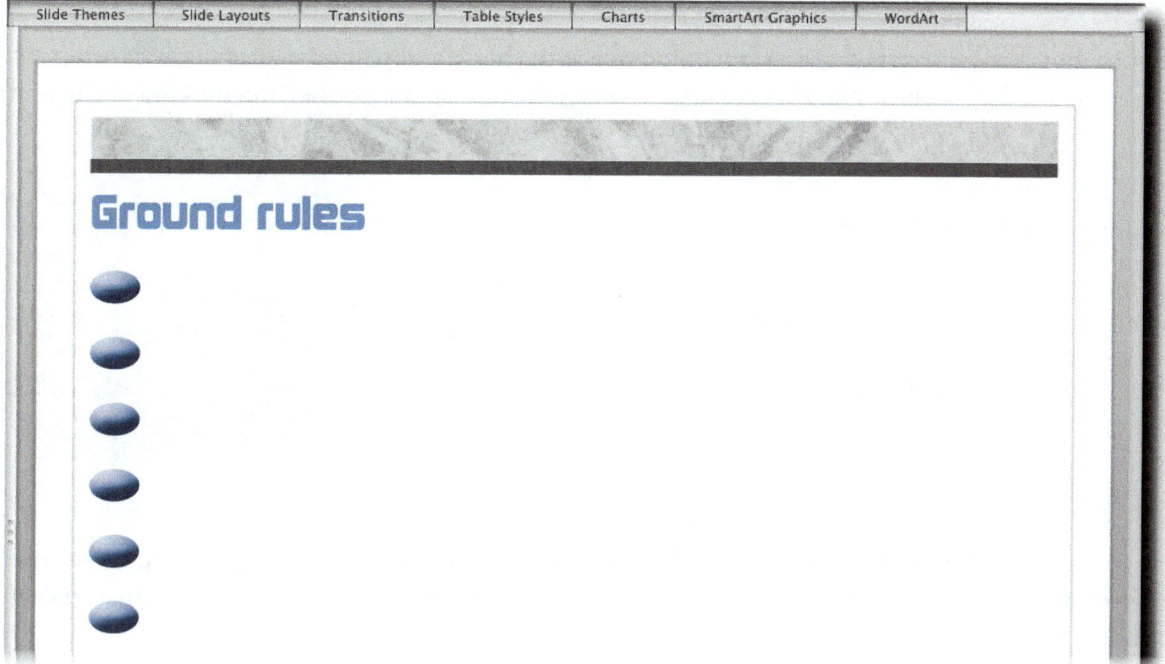

For more on presentations, see Unit 16.

13 Close your book. In pairs, brainstorm technical problems that might occur when you take part in a videoconference. Then complete the mind map with your ideas.

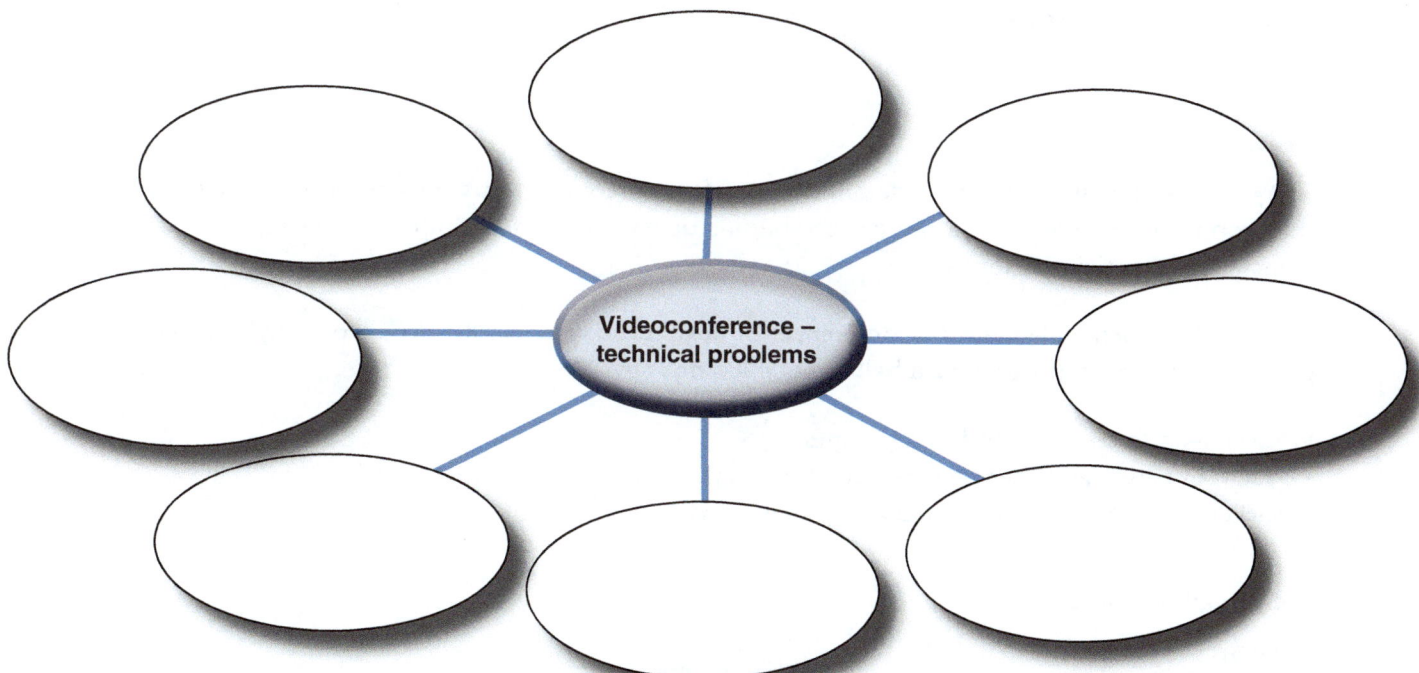

14 Now turn to Case study 11 on page 90 for more practice on talking about technical problems.

15 For a list of expressions from this unit, see Useful language Unit 11 on page 96.

Unit 12 Keeping the discussion on track

Background

In the previous unit Natasha opened the videoconference with the Tara distributors. Let's now continue with the meeting itself and look at how Natasha manages to keep the discussion focused and moving in the right direction.

> **Culture point – Staying focused**
> In some organizations participants in meetings naturally keep focused on the task in hand and the conversation stays 'on track'. In others, some participants regularly go off the point and need to be managed very carefully to ensure that the discussion has a clear focus. What experiences have you had of keeping meetings on track?

Skills work

1   Look at the email Natasha sent to the distributors about the videoconference. <u>Underline</u> the words and phrases that show that the email is very (even too) informal. Then compare your answers with a partner.

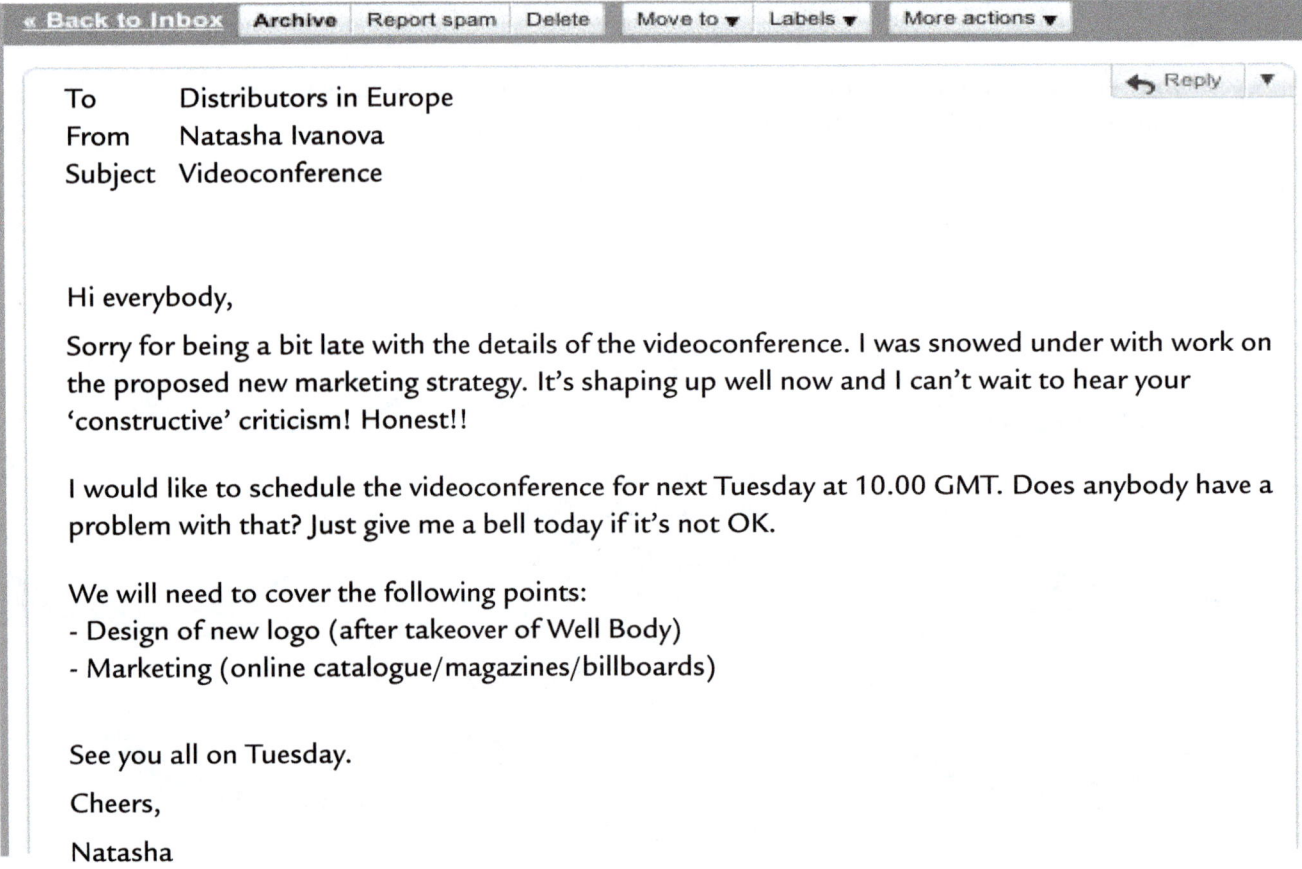

To   Distributors in Europe
From   Natasha Ivanova
Subject   Videoconference

Hi everybody,

Sorry for being a bit late with the details of the videoconference. I was snowed under with work on the proposed new marketing strategy. It's shaping up well now and I can't wait to hear your 'constructive' criticism! Honest!!

I would like to schedule the videoconference for next Tuesday at 10.00 GMT. Does anybody have a problem with that? Just give me a bell today if it's not OK.

We will need to cover the following points:
- Design of new logo (after takeover of Well Body)
- Marketing (online catalogue/magazines/billboards)

See you all on Tuesday.

Cheers,

Natasha

2   Write the informal words and phrases from the email in 1 next to their formal equivalents in the table below.

Formal	Very informal
1 I hope this is acceptable for all of you	Does anybody **have** a problem with that?
2 I was extremely busy	
3 I apologize for the delay	
4 I welcome your comments and suggestions	
5 Dear colleagues	
6 Best regards	
7 Contact me by telephone	
8 I look forward to meeting you all	
9 It is developing well	

For more on formal and informal written language, see Unit 3.

3   Imagine you need to organize a videoconference at work next month. Use the notes below to write an email to inform the participants of the details.

To do
Send email to all members of sales team:
- Videoconference, 14.00 GMT
- Update on sales figures and new products

To
From
Attachment
Subject

4   **30** Relax and listen to the discussion in the videoconference. How much did you understand?

5   **30** Listen again to the distributors' comments about the proposed new logo. Who thinks the following? Write the letter N (Nando), S (Stefan), R (Roger) or C (Carmen) next to each statement.

   1   The range of products has increased as a result of the takeover of Well Body. ____
   2   The main business of the company has not changed since the takeover. ____
   3   The company should not change the logo. (three people) ____ ____ ____
   4   The company will lose its share of the market if it changes its logo. ____
   5   The company should only change the colour of the logo. ____

6   **30** Listen again and tick the expressions of opinion that you hear. Remember, you must hear the exact expression to be able to tick it.

   1   I don't think that…   ☐   5   As I see it…   ☐
   2   I think…   ☐   6   In my opinion…   ☐
   3   I don't know how you feel but I think… ☐   7   Well personally, I think… ☐
   4   And I also think that…   ☐   8   If you ask me, I think…   ☐

Unit 12 Keeping the discussion on track

7 Rearrange the words to make sentences used to keep the discussion on track. The first one is done for you.

1 now. / Let's / into / not / go / that *Let's not go into that now.*
2 later. / We'll / to / that / on / come
3 get / I / want / don't / to / this / sidetracked / stage. / at
4 we / Can / later / that / please? / discuss
5 don't / I / want / get / to / the / off / point.
6 we / stick / Let's / to / logo / if / can. / the / at / moment / the

8 Match the pairs to make suggestions or recommendations.

1 Can I make   a move on?
2 I recommend we adapt   b about keeping the basic design?
3 How   c a suggestion?
4 I suggest   d should keep our old logo.
5 Shall we   e the logo.
6 I think we   f keeping the Tara logo.

9 Two managers are meeting to discuss a proposed new company logo. Read the beginning of their discussion and fill in the gaps with words from the box.

> suggestion   opinion   think   about   recommend   ahead

JACK: Can we start then by discussing the new logo?
JANE: I don't think there's much to discuss. In my ¹_____ the new design is perfect.
JACK: Do you really ²_____ so? Are you happy with the colour scheme?
JANE: Yes, I feel that the combination of red and pink is very effective.
JACK: Really? Can I make a ³_____ ?
JANE: Sure. Go ⁴_____ .
JACK: How ⁵_____ keeping the design but changing the colours? I ⁶_____ black on a white background.

Further practice

10 🔊31 Pronunciation practice. Listen to the correct sentences from exercises 7 and 8, and repeat them. Try to sound as natural as possible.

> **Key words**
> **core** (adjective): most important, or most basic
> **get sidetracked** (phrase): to have the progress of something delayed by people focusing on less important things
> **takeover** (noun): when one company takes control of another

11 Adverbs. Make the underlined word in each sentence stronger by adding a suitable adverb from the box. Each adverb may only be used once. The first one is done for you.

> very   completely   ~~fully~~   absolutely   strongly

1 I accept your point of view. *I fully accept your point of view.*
2 I'm against changing the logo.
3 I think the strategy is ridiculous.
4 I recommend it.
5 The meeting went well.

Over to you

12 Read this article from a business magazine about keeping meetings on track. Discuss the following with a partner:

- Which is the best tip? Which is the worst tip?
- What do you think of the approach described in the article? Too soft, too hard, or just right?
- How do you think people in the meetings you attend would react to this approach?

KEEPING EVERYBODY ON TRACK

Have you ever been in meetings where people were talking about everything apart from the items on the agenda? Maybe this happens too often? How can it be stopped? Well, if it only lasts for a short time, the best thing is to be very casual and say something like: *'OK guys, we're going a bit off track here. Let's focus on the agenda and the problem we need to sort out.'*

When participants have been off track for some time and don't appear even to be thinking of focusing on the objective of the meeting, say: *'This discussion seems to be outside the framework of our agenda. Shall we stop it now or include the topic under any other business?'*

If the discussion is completely off the point and has nothing to do with the agenda at all, try to get the group to realize this by saying: *'Could I have your attention please? I'm not sure that this discussion is on track. Can we agree to continue it now if it's important, otherwise put it on the agenda for another meeting? If most people agree that it's not important, then those engaged in it can be asked to continue it on another occasion.'*

Another common problem is people talking too much and not sticking to the time allocated to items on the agenda. What's the best thing to do in this case? Simply say: *'We are not sticking to our agreed timings. Shall we agree a new set of more realistic times?'* This simple request is a very powerful way of making people more aware that they should be brief!

13 Imagine you are chairing a videoconference about Tara's online marketing, but the discussion keeps going off track. Look at the participants' speech bubbles below – what would you say each time to bring the discussion back to the main topic?

I like all the suggestions for the online marketing catalogue, but I am completely against marketing Tara on billboards…

Carmen

I think the online marketing strategy is very good, but I don't like the proposed magazine advertising campaign…

Roger

In my opinion, the online magazine would not be cost-effective. I recommend we only advertise on billboards and in fashion magazines…

Stefan

14 Now turn to Case study 12 on page 91 for more practice on keeping the meeting on track.

15 For a list of expressions from this unit, see Useful language Unit 12 on pages 96 and 97.

Unit 13 Coping with strong disagreement

Background

Three years ago the American company National Paper (NP) bought a 50% stake in Elite Holdings (EH), a large Russian paper mill company. They formed a 50-50 joint venture with the aim of modernizing EH's four paper mills and expanding the production of paper and cardboard pulp in Russia. The board of directors consists of two Americans (senior executives at NP) and three Russians (joint owners of EH).

Culture point – 'Softening the blow'? In some cultures, top managers can make decisions which affect lots of people negatively, without considering the consequences. In others, managers try to 'soften the blow' by spreading the impact of negative decisions over time. What is the situation where you are? How sensitive are company managers to employees' needs?

Skills work

EH/NP Emergency Board Meeting 24 June

Board members: Boris Butikov, Andrej Smirnof, Michail Dolgich, Karl Gebhart, Jason Woodman

1. **32** Listen to Boris Butikov, one of the three Russian owners of Elite Holdings, opening a board meeting. Answer the questions.
   1. Why are they holding the meeting?
   2. What is the problem with the quarterly sales figures?
   3. What is the forecast for the next quarter?
   4. How would you describe Boris' mood?

2. Match the pairs to make sentences used to move things along quickly.
   1. We all know why we are   a start today.
   2. So straight   b any time.
   3. Let's not waste   c to the point.
   4. And we must   d to waste.
   5. There's no time   e having this meeting today.

   For more on opening meetings, see Units 8 and 18.

3. Read how the meeting continues on the next page, and fill in the gaps with phrases from the box.

   | decisive action | completely straight | firm proposal | rubber stamp | normal meeting |
   | small misunderstanding | effective meetings | completely against | in secret | |

54 Unit 13 Coping with strong disagreement

BORIS BUTIKOV: I have already had a couple of meetings with my Russian colleagues and we have a ¹_____ to put on the table. We think that it will be painful but it is the only way forward. We need to take ²_____ immediately.
KARL GEBHART: Don't get me wrong, Boris. I'm pleased that you've given this some thought but I'm not happy that you've already discussed this with your Russian colleagues before coming to this meeting.
BORIS BUTIKOV: We had our ³_____ and we–
KARL GEBHART: If you'll just let me finish! If I can just finish! What I'm trying to say is that I don't like the idea that you think you can come to this meeting with a proposal that you've put together ⁴_____ and expect us to ⁵_____ it! I disagree completely with that way of working!
BORIS BUTIKOV: I think there has been a ⁶_____ . I agree with you entirely that the place for discussion and debate is in these meetings. I couldn't agree with you more. I am ⁷_____ anything that would prevent that. We are a team. We work together as a team. I am all for teamwork!
KARL GEBHART: I hear what you're saying, but the problem is it doesn't match your actions. What you say is different from what you do. I'm not convinced that you're being ⁸_____ with us!
BORIS BUTIKOV: I think we are wasting our time talking like this. My reason for coming here with some firm proposals was to make our meeting more effective. I believe strongly in having ⁹_____ . That is the only reason I did it. I wasn't expecting–
KARL GEBHART: Sorry to interrupt you. Can I just say something? I'm not convinced by your argument. This isn't the first time we've had this sort of problem. Of course I see your point about effective meetings, but the trouble is…

4 Without looking at the conversation in 3, match the two halves to make 'agreeing' and 'disagreeing' sentences.

1 I disagree   a against that.
2 I agree with   b agree with you more.
3 I couldn't   c me wrong.
4 I'm completely   d by your argument.
5 I'm not convinced   e you entirely.
6 Don't get   f completely with that.

5 Rearrange the words to make sentences which express strong views.

1 I / wasting / we're / our / think / time / like / talking / this.
2 believe / I / having / strongly / effective / in / meetings.
3 convinced / I'm / not / you / us! / are / that / being / straight / completely / with
4 need / immediately. / We / to / decisive / take / action
5 isn't / had / the / first / time / This / this / we've / of / sort / problem.

6 🔵 **33** Listen to the proposal Boris puts forward for the Russian workers. Decide whether the statements are true or false.

1 Boris proposes to make staff cuts at all levels.
2 Jason Woodman thinks that large staff cuts will lead to strikes.
3 Jason Woodman doesn't think the workers would sabotage the mills.
4 The EH security staff are well-trained.
5 Michail Dolgich thinks there is not enough security.
6 Boris Butikov wants to fire half of the mill workers.
7 All staff who lose their jobs will get redundancy pay.

7 Read the sentences from the discussion. Who do you think says what? Write the letter B (Boris), A (Andrej), M (Michail), K (Karl) or J (Jason) next to each statement.

1 Sorry again about that misunderstanding. ____
2 You'll never get away with that! ____
3 We propose to fire 50% of the mill workers next Friday. ____
4 The main problem would be possible strikes. ____
5 We can control any staff problems. ____
6 Thanks for agreeing to go through our proposals. ____
7 We've got very well-trained security staff. ____
8 We've got enough security to protect the mills and deal with problems. ____
9 Sorry for cutting in again Boris, but there are lots of disadvantages too. ____

33 Then listen again and check your answers.

8 **34** Listen to Boris' plans for the American managers and engineers. Fill in the right-hand column of the table.

Number of American employees:	
Job titles (two answers):	
Length of contracts:	
Accommodation:	
Russian staff supporting each American (two answers):	
Number of redundancies:	

Further practice

9 Check the listening script for exercise 8, on page 103. In pairs, continue the conversation for three minutes. Read through the following notes carefully before starting the roleplay.

Student A: You are Karl Gebhart. React to Boris' plans for the American workers. You actually think the plans are realistic, as most of the workers are in the last year of their contracts and they are starting to get homesick (they miss home). Come to an agreement with Boris about how best to break the news to them.
Student B: You are Boris Butikov. Listen to Karl's reaction to your plans for the American workers. Come to an agreement with Karl about how best to break the news to them.

10 **35** Pronunciation practice. Listen to the following sentences and repeat them. Notice how the words in bold have the heaviest stress in each sentence.

There's **no** time to waste.
We need to take **decisive** action **immediately**.
I disagree **completely** with that.
I **couldn't** agree with you **more**.
I **strongly** believe in having **effective** meetings.
You'll **never** get away with that!

> **Key words**
> **board** (noun): the people in a company who make major decisions about the way it is managed
> **fire** (verb): to make someone leave their job, sometimes as a punishment
> **redundancy** (noun): when someone is told to leave their job because they are no longer needed
> **strike** (noun): a period of time when people refuse to work, in protest about something

11 **Present perfect. Make general comments about the past. The first one is done for you.**
   1 They / do / good job *They have done a good job.*
   2 He / have / difficulties adapting / Russian way of life
   3 We / not visit / American office
   4 They / decide / sack a lot of workers
   5 The American engineers / live / Russia / several years

Over to you

12 **Prepare answers to these questions and discuss them with a partner.**
   1 Have you ever been to a meeting where there was a lot of conflict and strong disagreement? How did you feel?
   2 Do you think it is possible for such meetings to be productive? Can they achieve their aims despite the arguments?

13 **Brainstorm with a partner the most common reasons for arguing in meetings. Then complete the mind map with your ideas.**

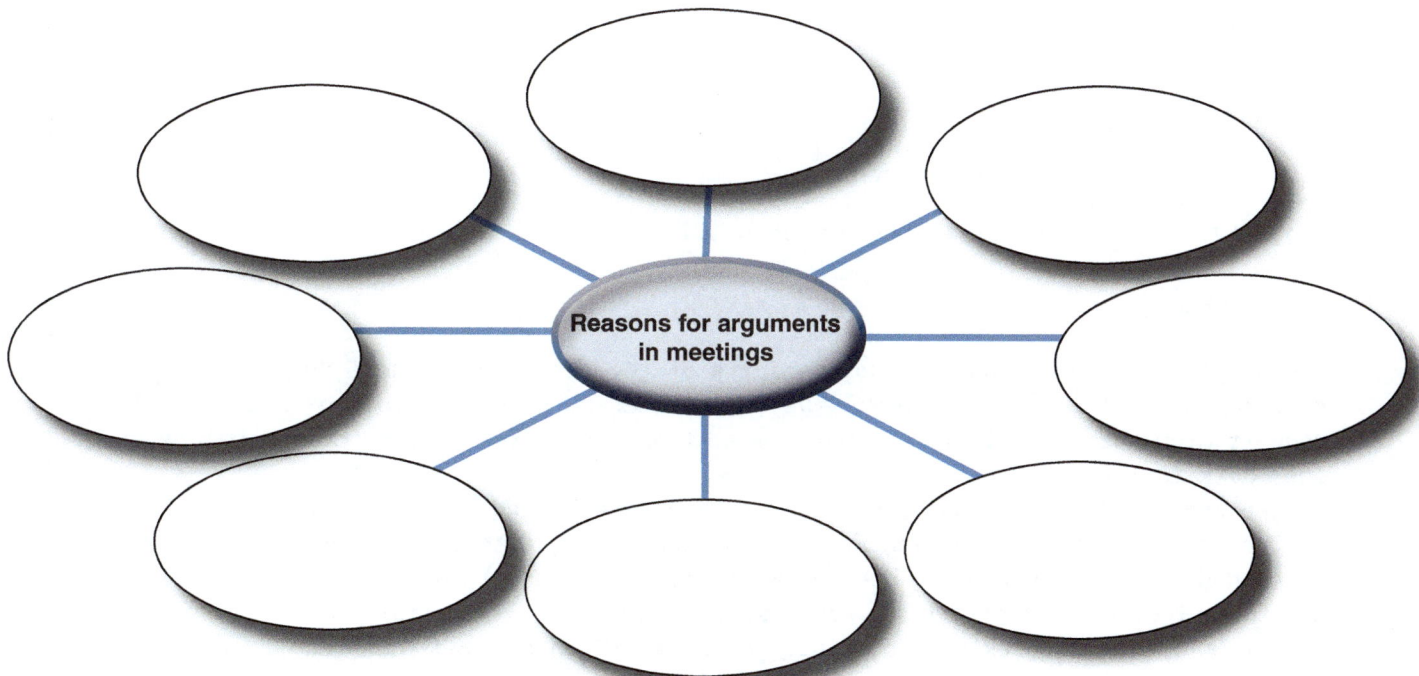

14 Now turn to Case study 13 on page 91 for a roleplay based on strong disagreement.

15 For a list of expressions from this unit, see Useful language Unit 13 on page 97.

Unit 13 Coping with strong disagreement

Unit 14 Dealing fairly and sensitively with difficult issues

Background

After the highly charged emergency board meeting in the last unit, Karl Gebhart now has to break the news about the cuts to the American employees working for the joint venture. Redundancy is an emotional issue whatever the company, so it is crucial that it is dealt with both fairly and sensitively.

Culture point – Managerial styles Some managers try to control or dominate the people who work for them, in order to show their power and authority. Others may take a more collaborative approach and try to involve their employees more. What is the situation where you are? Does your boss ask your opinion about issues relating to work?

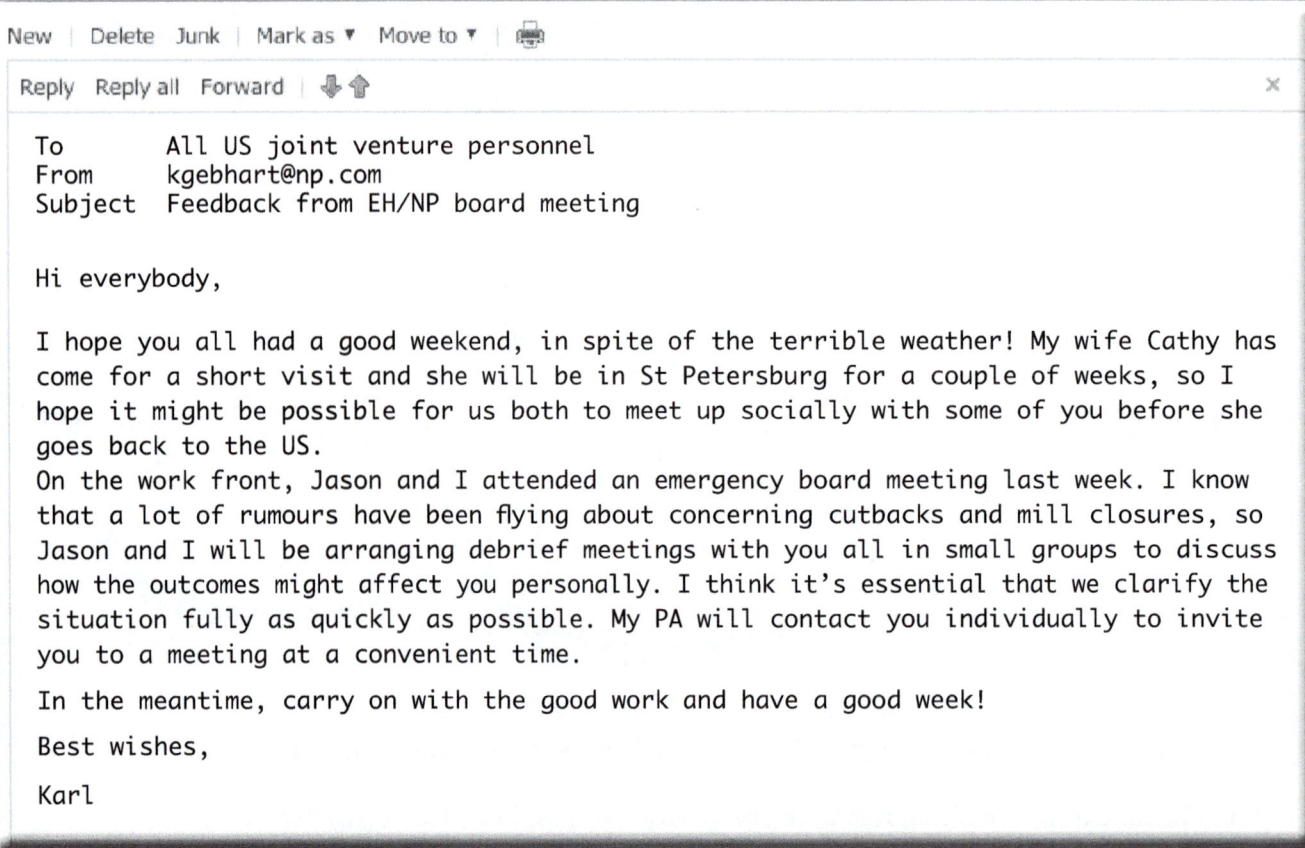

Skills work

1. Look at the email that Karl Gebhart sent to all of the American employees after the board meeting. Is his relationship with the staff formal or informal? Write your answer on the next page, giving examples from the email.

```
To        All US joint venture personnel
From      kgebhart@np.com
Subject   Feedback from EH/NP board meeting

Hi everybody,

I hope you all had a good weekend, in spite of the terrible weather! My wife Cathy has come for a short visit and she will be in St Petersburg for a couple of weeks, so I hope it might be possible for us both to meet up socially with some of you before she goes back to the US.
On the work front, Jason and I attended an emergency board meeting last week. I know that a lot of rumours have been flying about concerning cutbacks and mill closures, so Jason and I will be arranging debrief meetings with you all in small groups to discuss how the outcomes might affect you personally. I think it's essential that we clarify the situation fully as quickly as possible. My PA will contact you individually to invite you to a meeting at a convenient time.

In the meantime, carry on with the good work and have a good week!

Best wishes,

Karl
```

I think Karl's relationship with the staff is informal / formal (*cross out the one that doesn't apply*) because of the following expressions and topics in the email:

_____
_____
_____

For more examples of formal and informal language, see Unit 3.

2   Imagine you have to organize a meeting with your co-workers to give some bad or unpleasant news. Write an email similar to Karl's message in 1. Remember to:
   - write some 'small talk' at the beginning
   - mention the reason for meeting
   - give the details of when and where the meeting will take place
   - end the email positively.

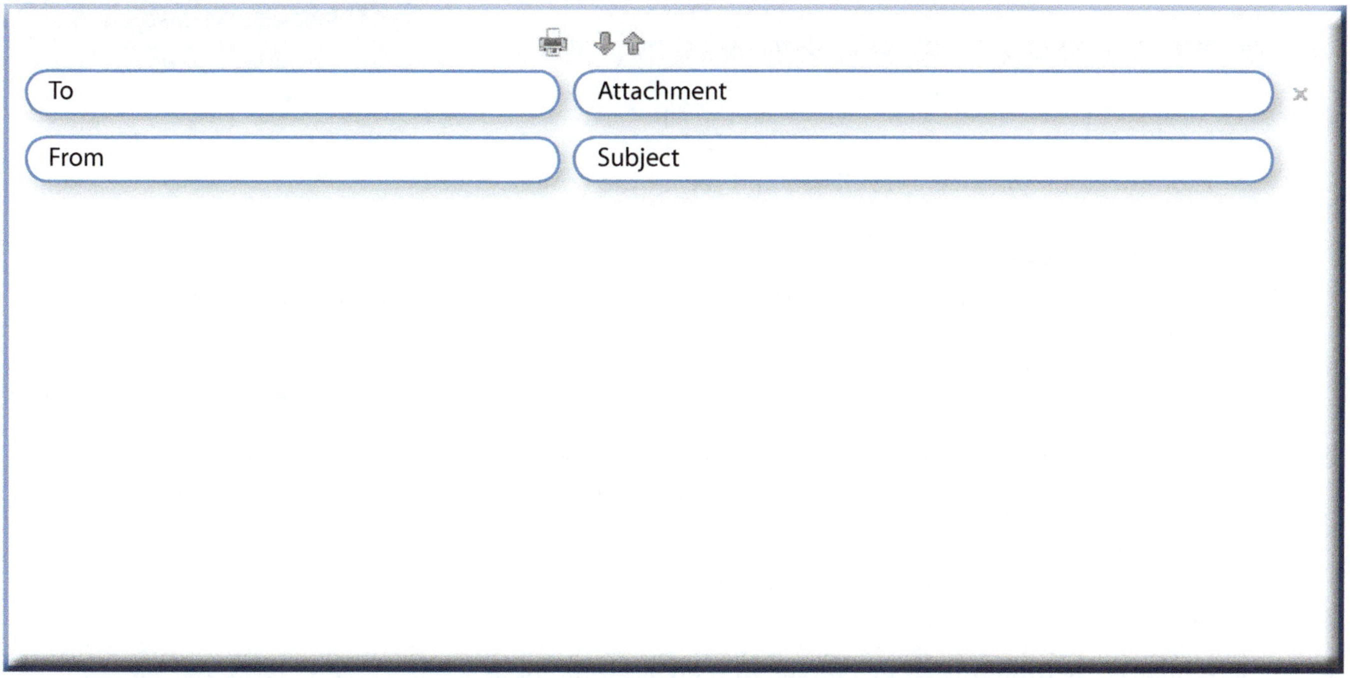

To	Attachment
From	Subject

3   36 Listen to part of a meeting between Karl and a manager and two engineers, all of whom work at the EH paper mill in Siberia. Karl has just finished telling them about the decision to cut staff. How do they react?

4   36 Look at the statements below, which give the participants' opinions in different words. Listen again to the conversation and write the initials AD (Andrew Driscol), TD (Tony Dando) or SP (Sam Pogue) next to the statements.
   1   He knows that the demand for paper pulp has decreased. ____
   2   He doesn't like the company's behaviour towards the Russian workers. ____
   3   He agrees with his two colleagues. ____
   4   He thinks the company's course of action is harsh. ____
   5   He thinks the company is not acting legally. ____
   6   He is shocked by how the company plans to deal with the problem. ____
   7   He knows that the financial situation is bad. ____
   8   He thinks the company is acting in an old-fashioned way. ____

5 Rearrange the words to make sentences that Karl uses to try to make people think positively.
1 on / Shall / try / we / and / the / focus / points? / positive
2 at / your / objective. / positively, / this / already / you've / achieved / Looking / main
3 look / at / in / ways. / You / it / can / two

6 Use the words in the box to complete the phrases Karl uses to bring people into the conversation.

| think | reaction | come | start | thoughts |

1 Can I get some _____ from you now?
2 Would you like to _____ ?
3 Could I ask you to _____ in now?
4 What do you _____ ?
5 What are your _____ ?

For more on inviting participants to speak, see Units 6 and 18.

Further practice

7 🔊 **37** Pronunciation practice. Now listen and repeat the sentences in 6.

> **Key words**
> **cut / cutback** (noun): a reduction in money or staff
> **debrief** (verb): to get information from someone who has just finished something important
> **outcome** (noun): the final result of a process or meeting
> **rumour** (noun): unofficial information that may or may not be true

8 Phrasal verbs. Match the phrasal verbs with the definitions.
1 lay off   a to recover from
2 come in   b to dismiss from a job
3 cut back   c to join the discussion
4 get over   d to reduce

9 Phrasal verbs revision. Listen to a production manager discussing a problem with his assistant. Complete the gaps with a phrasal verb from the box in the right form.

| go over | draw up | come up | get back | tie up | cut back | get in | sort out |

MANAGER: Sales are down, but I'd like to avoid ¹_____ our next print run. Can you ²_____ touch with the team and ³_____ a meeting?
ASSISTANT: I'll do it right away. And don't worry, we're a creative group – I'm sure we'll ⁴_____ with a solution.
MANAGER: OK, can you do that today and ⁵_____ to me by five o'clock?
ASSISTANT: Sure, no problem. I'll ⁶_____ an agenda and we can ⁷_____ the details together.
MANAGER: Great. I'd like to ⁸_____ all the loose ends before the end of the week.

Over to you

10 Close your book and in pairs, brainstorm tips for giving bad news. Make a note of the ideas as you think of them, and when you are finished, number them in order of importance (1=most important). Some examples have been given to start you off.

> **Tips for giving bad news**
> - Make sure you meet in a comfortable location.
> - Offer the person a cup of tea or coffee.
> - Ask a few friendly questions about his or her family.
> -
> -
> -
> -
> -
> -
> -

11 Read this article from a business magazine about how to give bad news to employees. Summarize the tips in your own words. Which is the best tip? Why?

Saying what needs to be said

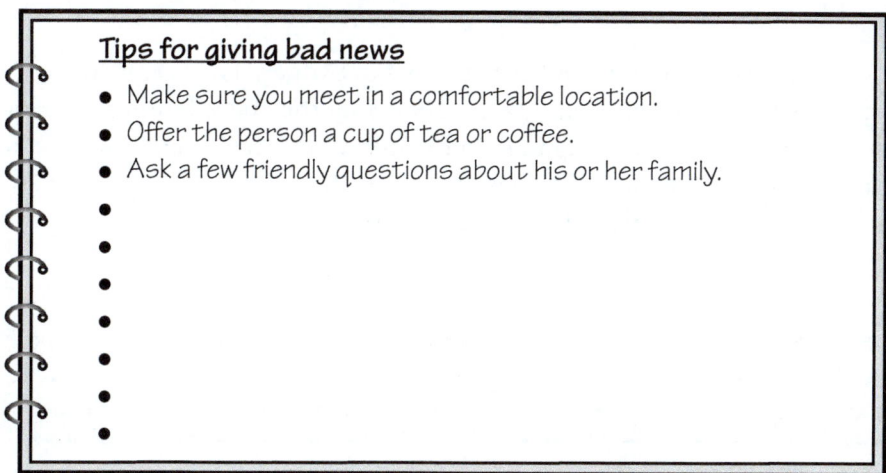

No manager looks forward ¹____ telling members of staff that they are fired, but it sometimes has to be done. So what is the best way to do it? Firstly, try to use as much gentle language as possible to soften the blow: opening the announcement with words/ phrases like 'Unfortunately', 'I'm sorry to say/tell you that' or 'It's with great regret that' can often make a great deal of difference.

Secondly, emphasize that it is the job that is being cut, not the person. Make sure you speak to each person individually and ²____ private, preferably at the end of the day on a Friday. This means that they can be asked to leave the company immediately without having the chance to damage any equipment or documents. It also means that they have the weekend to get ³____ the bad news.

It is also important that the lay-off should not be a complete shock to the individual, so after a general announcement has been made that the company has to cut ⁴____ on staff, it is a good idea to keep telling everybody that no job is protected – not even your own. This gives people the chance ⁵____ start planning for the future, as everybody will start wondering if this is the time to start looking for another job.

In addition, make it clear to everybody what benefits the company is offering ⁶____ everybody who is sacked. This could include a financial package, good references for their next job or career advice from the company's HR department. That can also sweeten the pill.

12 Fill in the gaps in the article in 11 with the missing prepositions.

13 Now turn to Case study 14 on page 91 for more practice on breaking bad news.

14 For a list of expressions from this unit, see Useful language Unit 14 on page 97.

Unit 14 Dealing fairly and sensitively with difficult issues

Unit 15 Taking part in a brainstorming meeting

Background

Ten Monkeys is an Australian advertising agency based in Sydney. They are a very successful company with a mixed and varied client base that they have built up over the last two decades. Their clients include famous names in banking, retailing, insurance, and the car and entertainment industries. Their latest contract has them working on a new website for Sanita, an international healthcare organization.

Culture point – Participation In some cultures there is a strong tradition of participation in meetings – especially in brainstorming, which needs everybody's full involvement to work properly. In other cultures participants are less willing to share their ideas unless specifically asked to do so. What is it like in meetings you go to or have been in?

Skills work

1   Read the email from Bill Kennedy, an experienced client services executive at Ten Monkeys, to his team. Answer the questions.

   1   How many people are in the team?
   2   Why is he organizing a meeting?
   3   When and where is the meeting?
   4   What does everybody have to do before the meeting?

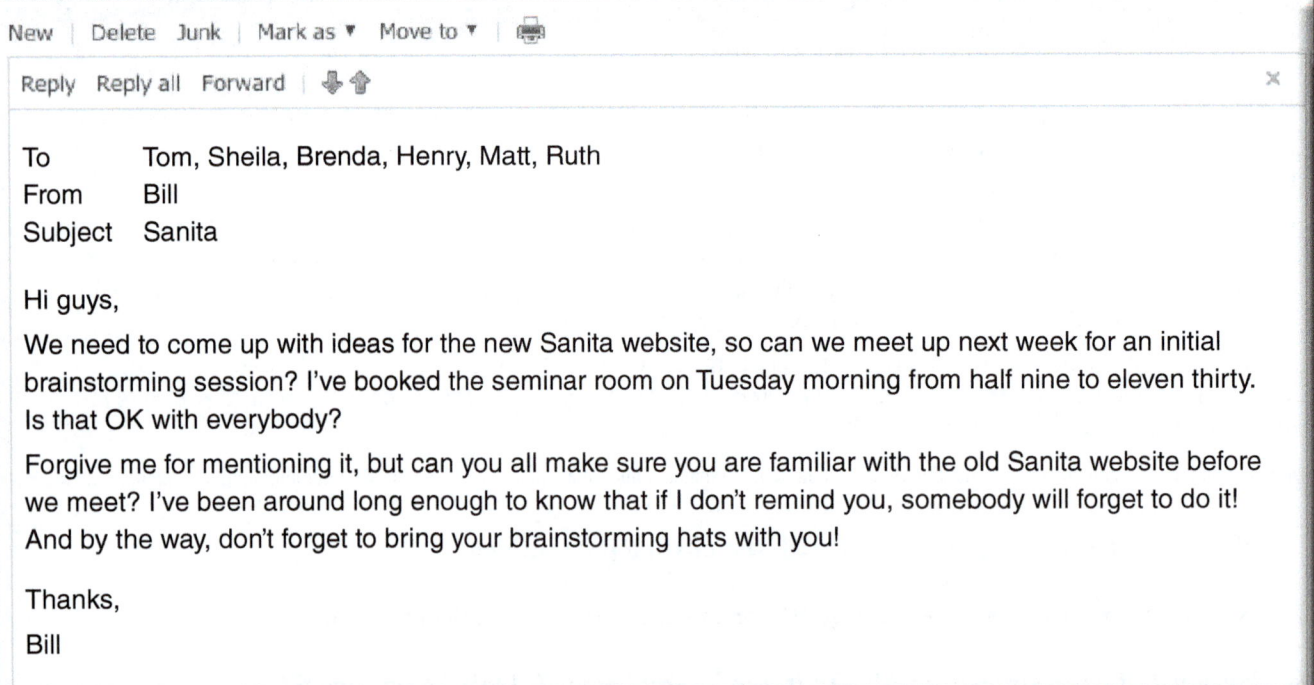

2   **38** Look at Bill's mind map, covering the features of Sanita's service that the new website might focus on. Then listen to the start of the brainstorming meeting. Write the features from the mind map on the bottom half of the flip chart, in the order in which they are discussed (1–10).

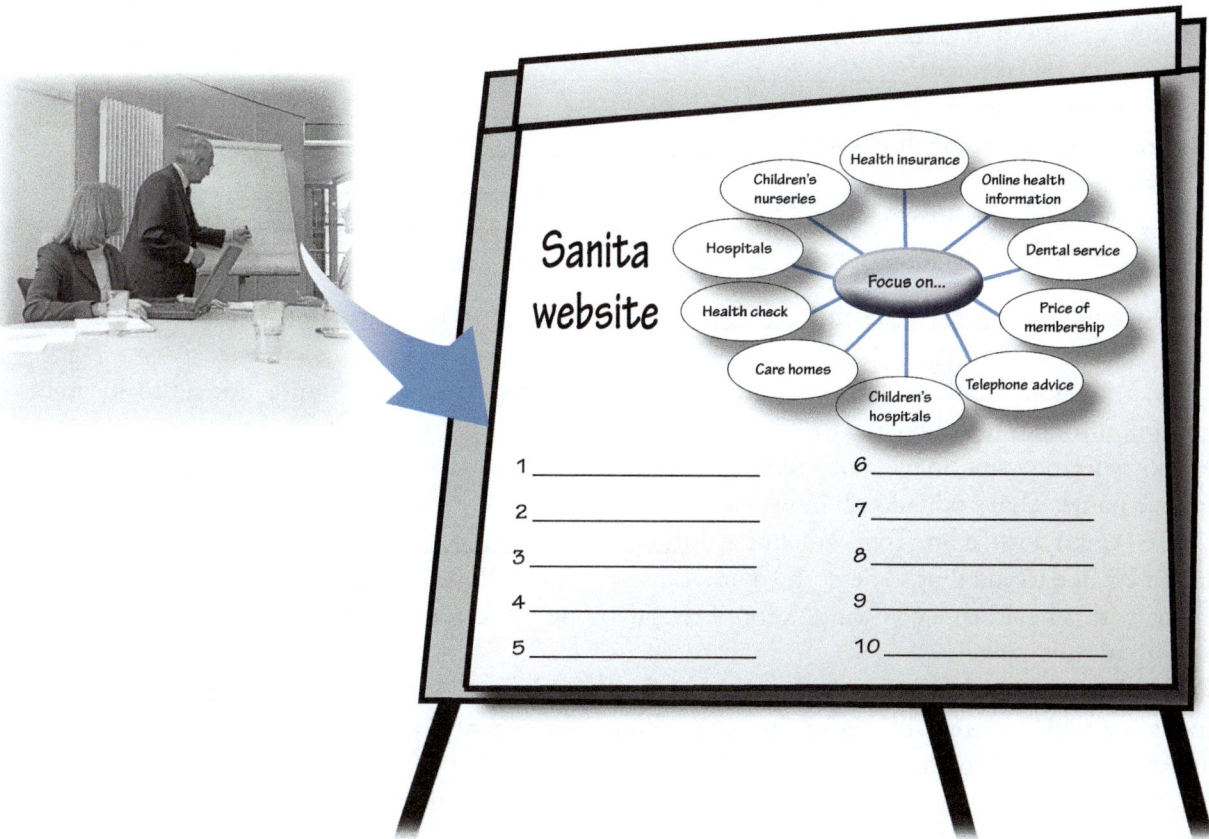

3   Rearrange the words to make sentences that Bill uses to clarify what has been said.
   1   highlight / So / we / services. / need / clarify, / to / the / range / wide / to / of
   2   come / Here's / we've / what / so / with / far. / up
   3   suggested / through / I'll / so / run / far. / just / what / we've

4   **39** Listen to check your answers to 3. Then repeat the sentences.

5   Match the pairs to make sentences which summarize what has been said. Check in the Useful language section (Unit 15) on page 97 if necessary.
   1   I'll just go   a   what we've suggested so far.
   2   Here's what we've come   b   through what we have suggested.
   3   I'll just run through   c   up with.
   4   I think we've come up   d   been suggested.
   5   I'll just summarize what has   e   with several major areas. Firstly,…

6   Imagine you are the chairperson. Use Bill's mind map in exercise 2, and new expressions from the unit, to help you do a spoken summary of the brainstorming meeting. Work in pairs, taking it in turns to be the chairperson.

Unit 15 Taking part in a brainstorming meeting

7 After the brainstorming session the team has a short break before reconvening to come up with some new ideas for revamping the image of Sanita. Read the discussion below and write the underlined sentences next to the different categories (1–8). The first one is done for you.

1 Expressing an opinion: _I think it sounds too clinical_
2 Making a suggestion: _____
3 Expressing disagreement: _____
4 Expressing agreement: _____
5 Interrupting to join the discussion: _____
6 Avoiding an issue: _____
7 Commenting on what somebody else has said: _____
8 Asking an open-ended question: _____

BILL: OK then, shall we have another go at pooling our ideas? This time I want us to focus on the image of Sanita.
SHEILA: You know, I'd like to jump in straight away and say that the name 'Sanita' doesn't really grab me! I think it sounds too clinical…too, er–
TOM: Sorry to interrupt Sheila, but I really don't think it's our job to start suggesting a change to the company's name. That's ridiculous!
BRENDA: Calm down a bit, Tom! You know, I think Sheila has a good point – and to back up her argument I'd like to add that some of the market research we've done confirms that people don't associate the name with a healthcare company. A lot of people thought the company produces sinks and toilets! Honest, that's not a joke!
BILL: I'd like to come in here and say I agree completely with Tom. My reason for saying that is that the company has traded successfully under the name 'Sanita' for over fifty years, twenty of which have been in partnership with Ten Monkeys and myself.
SHEILA: I'm really not convinced by that argument, Bill. That's really not how I see it! I can't see any advantage in keeping the company name. I only see disadvantages!
BILL: I wasn't really expecting the discussion to take this turn. I would really rather not talk about this issue at the moment. I don't think we have enough information from the market research to enable us to make sensible judgments on this matter. I suggest we come back to this later on at another meeting perhaps.
BRENDA: Sorry Bill, but I'm not really sure what you mean by that.
BILL: It just means that I would like us to focus on the main purpose of the meeting, not on side issues. OK, let's move on. Can you tell me your views on the suggested new logo for Sanita?

For more on opinions and disagreement, see Units 12 and 13.

Culture point – Age In some cultures people have to retire from work when they reach pensionable age, but in others people can continue to work until they are 70 or even older. What is it like in your country? How old is your boss? What do you think are the advantages and disadvantages of older people continuing to work?

Further practice

8 **40** Pronunciation practice. Listen to the following sentences and repeat them. Notice how the words in bold run into each other, often sounding like one word rather than three. Try to copy the pronunciation.

I don't **want to say** too much more at this stage.
Feel **free to help** yourself to a coffee from the machine.
It's important for **people to know** they can get help.
Over to you now, Brenda.

>
> Key words
>
> **client base** (noun): a group of people who use a particular service
> **pensionable** (adjective): officially old enough to stop work and receive a pension
> **pool** (verb): to share something such as money, ideas, equipment, etc
> **reconvene** (verb): to come together for another meeting

9 *Will + just* for spontaneous decisions. Write a spontaneous decision for each situation. The first one is done for you.

1 You need to summarize a discussion. *I'll just summarize the discussion.*
2 You need to go through the advantages and disadvantages of a proposal.
3 You need to clarify a point.
4 You need to say the main points again.

Over to you

10 Prepare answers to these questions.

1 Have you ever attended a brainstorming meeting? What did you brainstorm about?
2 In your opinion, what makes a really good brainstorming session?

11 Now interview other colleagues about their experience of brainstorming meetings. Make a note of their answers and report back your findings.

12 Discuss with a partner the advantages and disadvantages of brainstorming meetings. Comment on the ideas in the speech bubbles. For any disadvantages, try to think of ways to overcome the problem.

- Brainstorming is OK if everybody is confident.
- Some people are too shy to make much of a contribution.
- Brainstorming is fine if you think very quickly.
- It doesn't make sense to accept all ideas in a brainstorm.
- Some people interrupt the flow of ideas and want to discuss suggestions.
- Some people need to put their ideas on paper first.
- Some people like the sound of their own voice and dominate the brainstorm.
- Brainstorming is fantastic because it produces lots of new ideas.

13 Now turn to Case study 15 on page 92 to put your brainstorming skills into practice.

14 For a list of expressions from this unit, see Useful language Unit 15 on page 97.

Unit 16 Reporting back to the client

Background

In the previous unit we saw Bill and his team at Ten Monkeys starting work on a new website for their client, the healthcare organization Sanita. It is now time for Bill to contact Sanita about a prototype version of their website that the Ten Monkeys team have been working on.

Culture point – 'The customer is king' The customer is 'king' (or queen) in most cultures because they pay the bill. They can usually say what they want, when and how. In some cultures, however, customers can sometimes ask for too much. What is the situation like in your country?

Skills work

1 Look at the email exchange between Bill and Sandra Buckingham, Sanita's marketing director, about the new website. Answer the questions.

  1 Is the relationship between Bill and Sandra more formal or informal? Justify your answer with examples from the emails.
  2 Where will the meeting take place?
  3 Who from Sanita will attend the meeting?
  4 Why do you think Bill prefers to bring his own IT equipment?

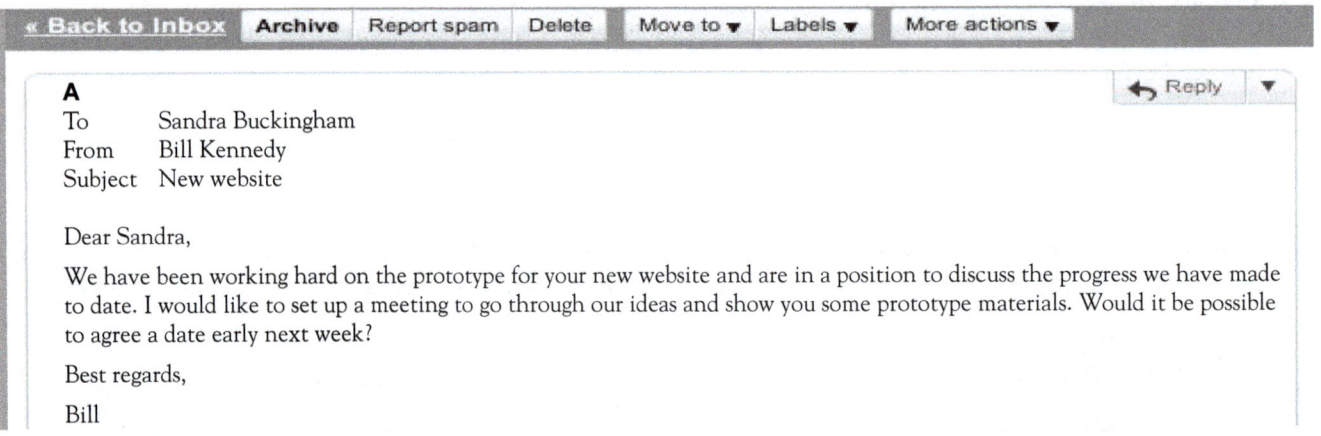

A
To   Sandra Buckingham
From   Bill Kennedy
Subject   New website

Dear Sandra,

We have been working hard on the prototype for your new website and are in a position to discuss the progress we have made to date. I would like to set up a meeting to go through our ideas and show you some prototype materials. Would it be possible to agree a date early next week?

Best regards,

Bill

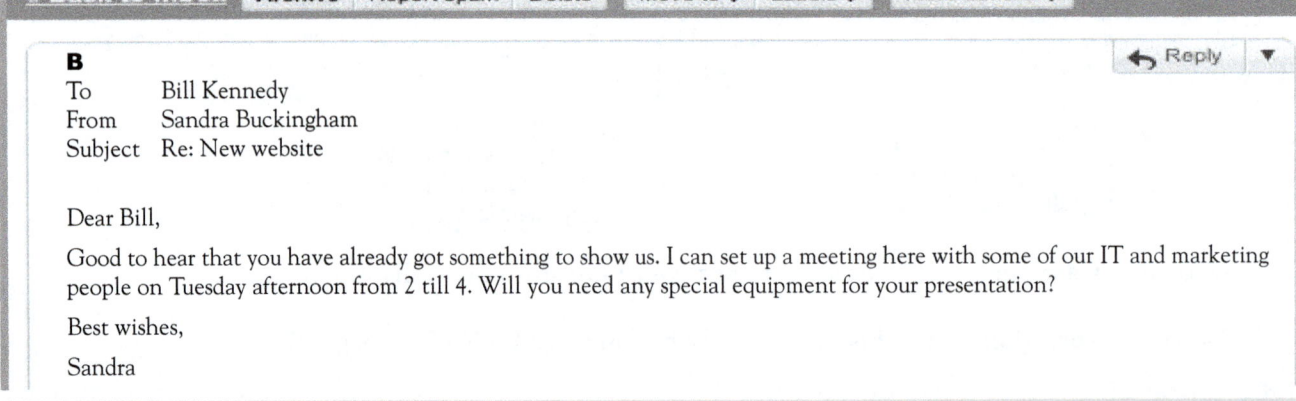

B
To   Bill Kennedy
From   Sandra Buckingham
Subject   Re: New website

Dear Bill,

Good to hear that you have already got something to show us. I can set up a meeting here with some of our IT and marketing people on Tuesday afternoon from 2 till 4. Will you need any special equipment for your presentation?

Best wishes,

Sandra

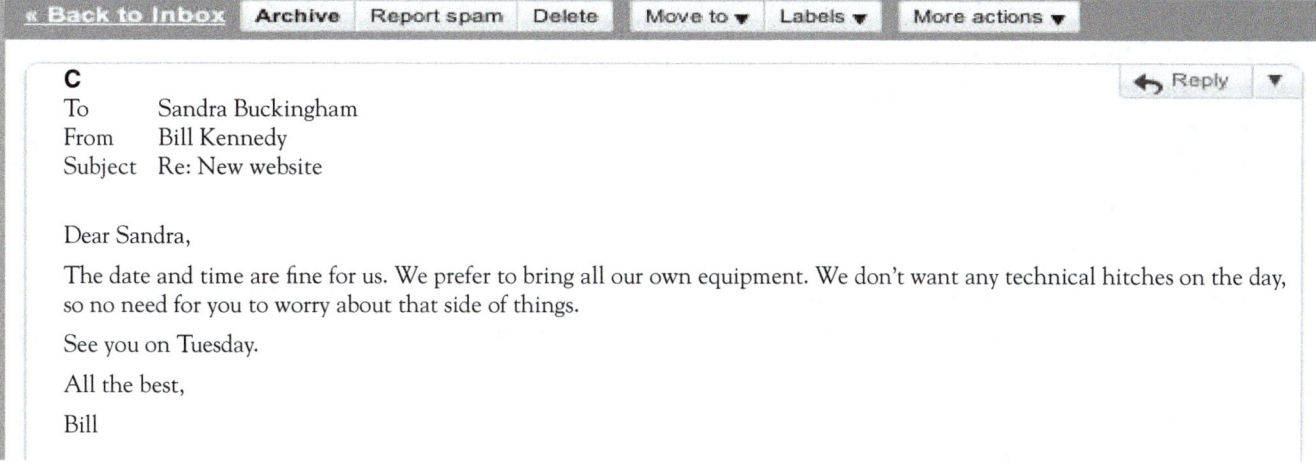

2 **41** Listen to Bill opening the meeting at Sanita. Decide whether the statements are true or false.
1 His presentation will be quite short.
2 There is a lot to talk about.
3 He wants to show some sample material for the website.
4 He is happy to receive feedback.
5 He says the sample home page is of high quality.
6 He would prefer to take questions at the end of the presentation.

3 Look at the following sentences which Bill then says to begin his presentation about the home page. Put them in the order that you think he says them. The first one is done for you.
a The order should reflect what the customer is most likely to be interested in. ___
b We spent a lot of time looking at the old home page and decided that it contained a lot of interesting information about your products and services. _1_
c So to sum up, what we propose is to make sure that the first page that the customer sees has more impact. ___
d In fact, we thought there was too much material on it. ___
e Moreover, the material didn't seem to be arranged in any priority order. ___
f It was confusing and just too dense. ___

4 **42** Listen to the next part of the presentation. In what ways is the home page shown below different from the one Bill describes?

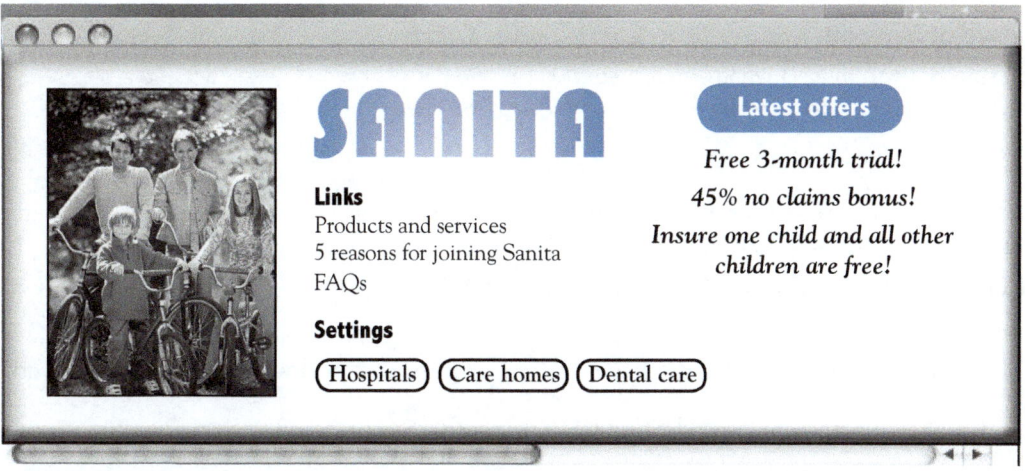

Unit 16 Reporting back to the client   67

5 Choose the correct words to make sentences connected with making things clearer.
1. Can I just ask you to run / walk through that again, please?
2. Could you tell us a little bit / little more about that?
3. What I'm trying / wanting to say…
4. I'll go over / under that again.
5. Let me place / put it another way…
6. Does that clear / clarify things?

6 Read these tips on making presentations in meetings. Are they all good advice? Discuss them with a partner and add a number to the beginning of each tip to reflect their importance (1=most important, 8=least important).

___ **Keep your visuals simple**
Don't have too many words on your posters, charts, flip chart pages or PowerPoint presentation. The people listening want to hear YOU, not read your notes!

___ **Make good eye contact with the audience**
Don't just look at one person. Make sure that you make good eye contact with several people throughout the presentation. Remember that you are talking to a group, not one individual.

___ **Don't be a robot!**
Let the audience see that you are a human being with a personality, not a machine presenting a list of boring facts. Try to get across a bit of individuality in your presentation.

___ **Make them laugh**
This does not mean you have to tell jokes! A simple and appropriate amusing remark will do. People are more relaxed and receptive when they laugh.

___ **Don't talk AT your audience**
Nobody wants to listen to a long, boring lecture. Try to create a dialogue with the audience. Ask them questions, as well as encouraging them to ask you questions.

___ **Tell the truth!**
If you don't know the answer to a question, say so and promise to find out and let them know later. The audience will appreciate your honesty and willingness to find the answer.

___ **Don't just learn your presentation by heart**
Of course you have to be well-prepared, but try to make your presentation sound natural, rather than a speech you have memorized.

___ **Move it! Move it! Move it!**
Try to move a bit (but not too much!) when you are speaking. Move your arms a bit, walk around a bit. Remember that people are more likely to be interested in a lively speaker.

7 Work in pairs. Imagine you are Bill and your partner is a Sanita representative. Tell your partner about the new home page. Remember to keep checking that your presentation is clear and that he/she understands. Remember to use the tips in 6, and to do the following:
- First, say a few things about the old home page.
- Then talk about the changes to the home page. (What is on it now and what has been removed.)

When you have finished, swap roles and do the activity again.

Further practice

8 **43** Pronunciation practice. Listen to the following sentences and decide whether the speaker's voice goes up or down at the end of the sentence. The first two are done for you.

1 Is that clear to everybody? *Up*
2 It's good to be back with you again. *Down*
3 That's a pretty damning criticism of our current home page, Bill!
4 Any questions so far?
5 Let me put it another way.
6 Does that clarify things?

Then repeat the sentences with the same intonation.

> **Key words**
> **demanding** (adjective): needing a lot of attention and not easily pleased or satisfied
> **prototype** (noun): the first form of something new, made before it is produced in large quantities
> **sample** (noun): an example or small amount of something that shows you what all of it is like
> **visuals** (noun): things such as drawings or photographs that help to explain something

9 Past simple. Complete the sentences with the past simple form of the verbs in brackets.

1 We _____ a lot of time looking at the home page. (spend)
2 We _____ that it _____ a lot of information. (decide, contain)
3 We _____ there _____ too much material. (think, be)
4 _____ they _____ to know the cost? (want)
5 She _____ _____ with the proposal. (not agree)

Over to you

10 Prepare answers to these questions.

1 Do you ever have to meet clients or customers to talk about the services your company can offer, or to report on the progress you are making on a project?
2 Have you ever had any 'perfect' customers, or particularly demanding ones?

11 Now interview other colleagues about their experience of dealing with clients or customers. Make a note of their answers and report back your findings.

12 Work in small groups. Prepare, and then make, a short presentation on one of the following topics, or another topic of your choice.

- a project you are currently working on
- a project you have recently completed
- your company's products or services

For more on talking about yourself, see Unit 9.

13 Now turn to Case study 16 on page 92 for more practice on making presentations to clients.

14 For a list of expressions from this unit, see Useful language Unit 16 on page 97.

Unit 17 Ending a meeting

Background

 Veronica Spitz is the Managing Director of IconOne Productions. The company makes documentary films about the UK and the British way of life for Japanese television. Over the last ten years she has produced documentaries on a wide range of topics ranging from the Royal Ballet to coastal erosion.

Culture point – Managing time Some chairpeople are good at ensuring that all the items on the agenda are covered in the allocated time, with a summary of the main points and AOB at the end. Other meetings can be less well-organized, sometimes lasting too long and not being concluded satisfactorily. What is it like where you are from?

Skills work

1 44 Listen to part of a meeting between Veronica and the directors of the television channel NPTV, in which they plan the documentary films that IconOne Productions will produce next year. In what order are the pictures below mentioned?

a   b   c

2 44 Listen again and decide if the sentences are true or false. For those that are false, say why.
   1 Veronica thinks it's a good idea to summarize what has been discussed.
   2 Three projects have been contracted for next year.
   3 The documentary about weddings will be forty minutes long.
   4 Veronica agrees to do the research for the wedding documentary by 13th January.
   5 The Japanese directors like costumes and traditions.
   6 They plan to make a short film on the life of the writer Rudyard Kipling.
   7 They want to film in the Kipling family home in the north of England.
   8 It might be expensive to film in Kipling's family house.
   9 They would also like to do a documentary about an open-air museum.
   10 They would like to film in the Black Country Museum near London.

3 Complete sentences 1–8, relating to summarizing and action points. The first letter of each word has been given.
   1 I think it's best if I just run through the m_____ points we've agreed.
   2 It's always better to s_____ decisions formally.

70   Unit 17 Ending a meeting

3 I think we have come up with two, possibly three, p_____ .
4 Firstly, we've agreed that we'll make a 30-minute d_____ .
5 My first job then is to r_____ some unusual situations...
6 ... and get back to you by the end of January with the ideas for your a_____ .
7 I should be able to give you an a_____ by the end of next week.
8 OK, that brings us to the l_____ point.

🔊 44 Then listen again to check your answers or add any that you didn't know.

4 Rearrange the words to make sentences used to confirm what has been discussed or decided.
1 decided / We've / produce / to / documentaries. / three
2 I / covers / that / the / main / decided. / think / points / have / that / been
3 confirm / I / we / want / that / to / about / a / film / Rudyard / Kipling. / make
4 are / It / that / we / all / weddings. / decided / seems / to / make / a / about / documentary
5 confirm, / to / Just / the / will / documentary / 30 / be / long. / minutes
6 our / that / the / points / main / of / think / discussion. / I / covers
7 you'll / the / research / So / do / the / by / month? / of / the / end

5 🔊 45 Listen and read the dialogue at the end of the meeting. Answer the questions.

CHAIRMAN: OK, that brings us to the end of all the items on the agenda. Are there any further points you would like to discuss? Is there any other business for the meeting?
VERONICA: Yes, under any other business I'd like to talk about accommodation and travel expenses for the camera crews. Is that possible?
CHAIRMAN: Yes, it's possible, but I think that's something we can sort out by email. Could you send me a few details and I'll get back to you as soon as I can.
VERONICA: Yes sure, no problem. I've already written a report about it. I can send you a copy at the end of the meeting.
CHAIRMAN: Fine. OK then, if there's nothing else to discuss I'd like to fix a date for our next meeting with Veronica. I think the best thing would be to organize a videoconference at the end of January to see where we are with the projects. Veronica, can you manage the 30th of January?
VERONICA: Yes, that's fine for me.
CHAIRMAN: Is that date OK for everybody else? Yes? OK, I would suggest that we start the conference at 6am GMT. A good early start for you, Veronica!
VERONICA: Don't worry about me. I understand the difficulties with the time difference only too well!
CHAIRMAN: And I assume that time is convenient for everybody else? OK? I think we've covered everything, so if nobody has anything to add I think we can stop there. It just remains for me to thank Veronica for her excellent contribution, as usual. I look forward to seeing you again at the next videoconference. Have a safe journey home.

1 What does Veronica want to discuss under AOB?
2 Why does the chairman not want to discuss Veronica's point under AOB?
3 What sort of meeting does the chairman want with Veronica in January?
4 Why do you think it is sometimes difficult for Japanese companies to communicate by phone or video link with the UK?

Further practice

6   Pronunciation practice. Now listen and repeat the correct sentences in exercise 3. Try to sound as natural as possible.

> **Key words**
> **allocate** (verb): to officially give something (eg time, a job) to someone or something else
> **approval** (noun): official agreement or permission
> **conclude** (verb): to end something, especially by doing or saying something
> **convenient** (adjective): easy to do, or not causing problems or difficulties

7   First and second conditional. Join the two phrases together to make sentences in the first and second conditional. The first one is done for you.
   1   we want to film there / we need to get permission
       If we want to film there, we'll need to get permission. (first conditional)
       If we wanted to film there, we'd need to get permission. (second conditional)
   2   I meet them / I try to persuade them
   3   we can manage it / that look really spectacular
   4   they not give their approval / the filming have to take place somewhere else

Over to you

8   Prepare answers to these questions and discuss them with a partner.
   1   Have you ever been involved in a meeting that took longer than it was supposed to? Why did this happen?
   2   What tips would you give a chairperson to ensure that a meeting ends correctly and on time?

9   Fiona Grant is a management consultant. Read what she says about how to end a meeting. Work with a partner and decide which points you agree with.

> I think that before you end a meeting you must review what you have done or achieved. So you need to provide a summary of what was decided and then outline the action that must be taken after the meeting. I try not to finish any discussion in a meeting without deciding on an action point. I also think it's crucial to determine who is going to do what and by what deadline. But the most important thing for me is to finish the meeting on time. Don't let it drag on forever. Don't go into detail that can be dealt with at another time or by email. If somebody asks a question at the end of the meeting that needs a long answer or a lot of discussion, tell him or her that you'll put it on the agenda for the next meeting or say that you will answer the question one-to-one after the meeting. Let's be honest, some participants like the sound of their own voices and try to use 'any other business' as a chance to show how eloquent they are. I find it better to ask for AOB points at the start of the meeting and only discuss them if there is time. And even then, I put the AOB points into priority order and set a short time limit for each one.
>
> I also like to spend the last few minutes of every meeting focusing on a couple of key questions to evaluate the meeting. For example, I might ask: What worked well? How can we improve the next meeting?
>
> Last but not least, I always set the date and time of the next meeting before people leave. This can save hours of telephoning and emailing after the meeting!

10 Find words in Fiona's text which mean the same as the following.
   1 summarize *(verb)*
   2 articulate *(adjective)*
   3 debate *(noun)*
   4 accomplished *(verb, past participle)*
   5 assess *(verb)*
   6 decide *(verb)*

11 Complete the left column of the pad with notes on the main points of Fiona Grant's advice in 9. Then, working in pairs and using your notes as support, take it in turns to make a presentation on how to end meetings successfully. When listening to your partner's presentation, use the right column of the pad to make notes about it and then give feedback. Use the example ideas on the pad to start you off.

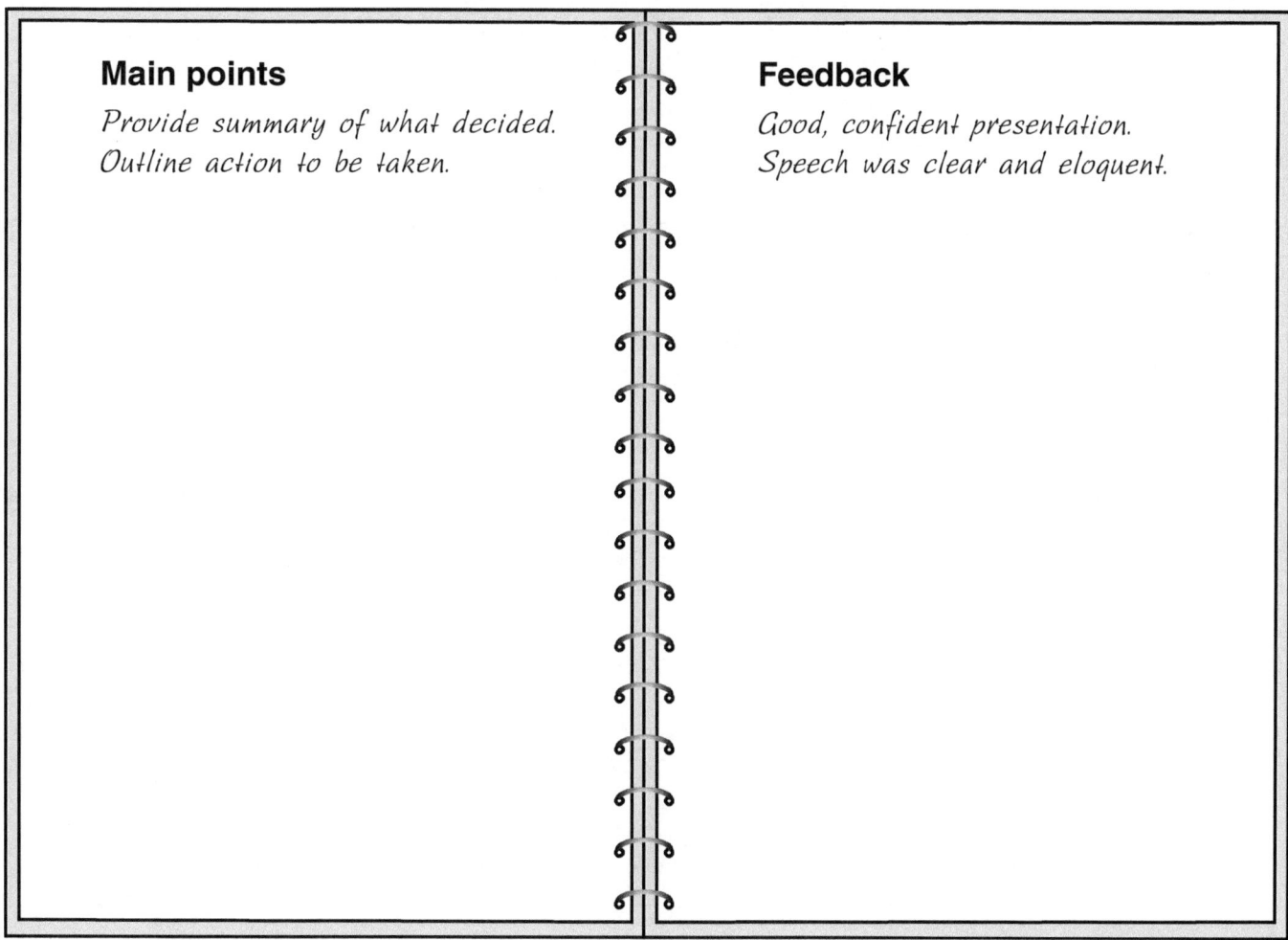

Main points
Provide summary of what decided.
Outline action to be taken.

Feedback
Good, confident presentation.
Speech was clear and eloquent.

For more on presentations, see Unit 16.

12 Now turn to Case study 17 on page 92 for a discussion activity on common problems at the end of meetings.

13 For a list of expressions from this unit, see Useful language Unit 17 on pages 97 and 98.

Unit 18 A formal board meeting

Background

Move It is an international sports club company with its head office in Milan. It has a network of sports clubs throughout Europe and is now planning to expand into South America and Asia. Most of the clubs are run on a franchise basis. The Move It board of directors consists of one representative from each country where it has more than twenty clubs.

Culture point – Protocol In some cultures there are strong traditions of very formal business meetings with strict procedures and protocol. What is it like in your culture? Do you have very formal meetings in your company? Do some participants find it difficult to use the correct language or wear the right clothes in very formal meetings?

Skills work

1   Read the invitation to the Move It board meeting and answer the questions.

   1   Where will the meeting take place?
   2   Why is the meeting important?
   3   Why does the president's PA need flight details?
   4   Will the participants have enough time to prepare for the meeting? Why? / Why not?

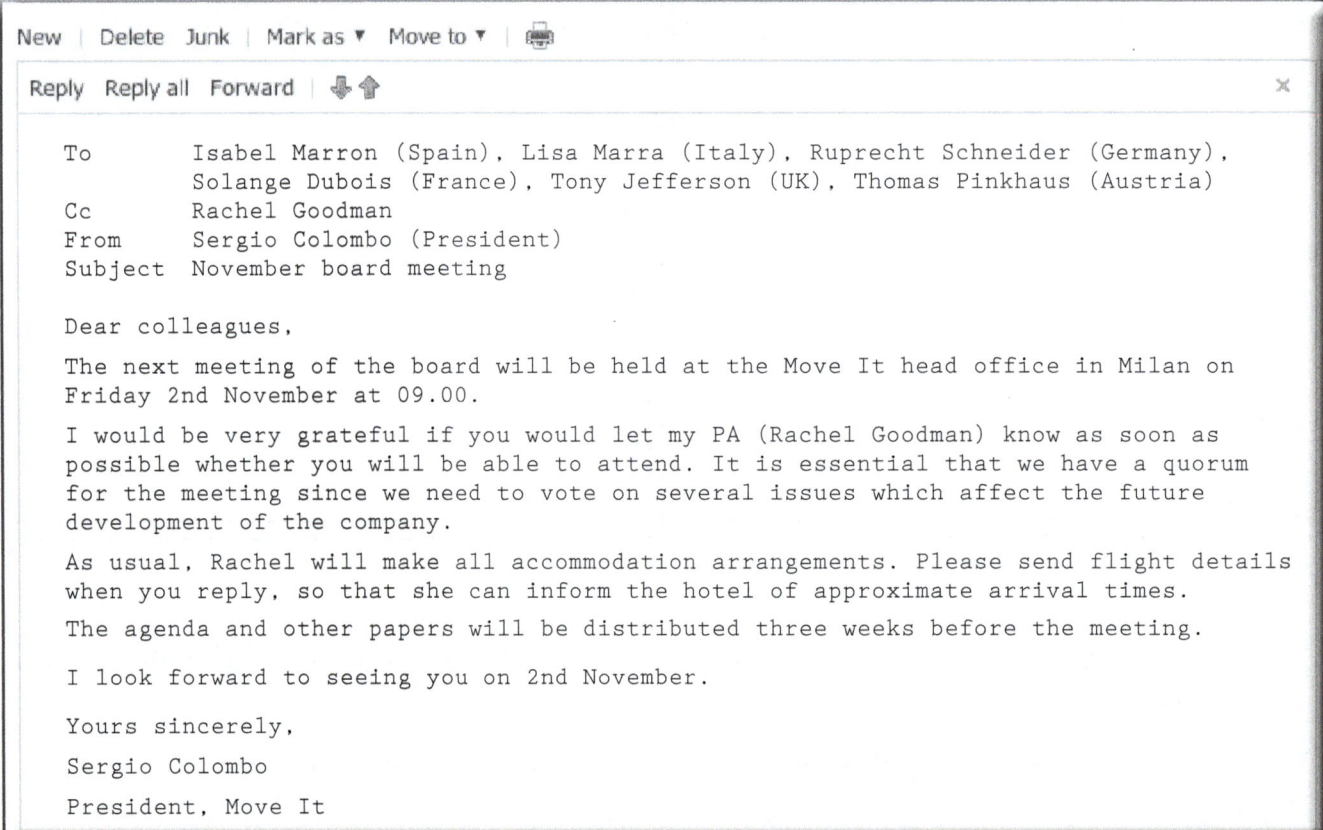

2   **47** Listen and read the beginning of Move It's formal board meeting, in which votes are taken on important decisions. Write the underlined words and phrases from the dialogue alongside the correct definitions (1–7).

1   The written record of a meeting. _____
2   The minimum number of participants present at a meeting in order to make a vote valid. _____
3   The final date by which something should be completed or achieved. _____
4   The list of decisions taken at the meeting which have to be completed. _____
5   Messages from people who say they are sorry that they cannot attend the meeting. _____
6   The chair asks for these to check that action points from the previous meeting have been completed. _____
7   When people who cannot attend a meeting ask somebody else to decide things for them. _____

PRESIDENT: Good morning everybody. I'm delighted to see so many of you present. As I mentioned in my email, it's crucial that we have a <u>quorum</u> today because we have to make some very important decisions affecting the expansion of the company in South America and Asia over the next two years. Firstly though, a few administrative matters. We have <u>apologies</u> from Tony Jefferson and Isabel Marron. They are both unwell but have authorized two other colleagues to make their <u>proxy votes</u> on the franchise applications. OK then. Can I sign the <u>minutes</u> of the last meeting as a correct record?
SOLANGE: I'm not sure, but I think there may be a small error on page 1. Item 2. I think we agreed to take action in December, not in March next year.
PRESIDENT: Thanks for that, Solange. Yes, I think you're right. That's how I remember it as well. Does everybody else agree? Yes? OK. Can you make the change, Rachel? OK then. May I sign the minutes now? OK? Thanks. And are there any <u>items arising</u> from the minutes?
RUPRECHT: I can report that all <u>action points</u> have been carried out by the required <u>deadline</u>.
PRESIDENT: Thanks very much, Ruprecht. That's very helpful. OK, I think we can start...

3   **48** Read the agenda. Then listen to the continuation of the meeting and circle the item on the agenda (1–7) that they are discussing.

```
Meeting of the Move It Board of Directors
Agenda
Objective       To consider applications for franchises in South America and Asia
Venue           Move It head office, Milan
Date and time   2nd November, 09.00
Participants    Move It directors
Apologies       Tony Jefferson (UK) and Isabel Marron (Spain)

Item 1 Report on the visit to clubs in Chile and Argentina
Item 2 Report on the franchise applications from Hong Kong and Beijing
Item 3 Report on the franchise applications from Tokyo and Osaka
Item 4 Acceptance or rejection of applications
Item 5 AOB
Item 6 Points for action
Item 7 Date of the next meeting
```

Unit 18 A formal board meeting

4 🔊48 Listen again and match the pairs to make sentences inviting participants to speak.

1	Who would	a	come in now?
2	Could we hear	b	like to start?
3	Who else would like	c	a few words?
4	Maybe you'd like to	d	to come in at this point?
5	Would you like to say	e	the Italian perspective from you?

For more on bringing people into the conversation, see Units 6 and 14.

5 🔊49 Thomas Pinkhaus uses quite a lot of informal language in this discussion. Listen to him again and complete the informal words and phrases 1–6 in the text. Then match them with the definitions (a–f) below. The first one is done for you.

'¹About ___time___ , I thought you were never going to ²get _____ to me! Well, our Lisa here is ³a smart _____ and she has made a few good points. ⁴_____ , I think the health and safety issues about the premises in Chile and Argentina are a ⁵_____ great problem. But you know, the situation in Asia as Lisa has just said is much better. It would ⁶_____ be good to hear what my fellow directors think.'

a informal word for 'yes' ___
b certainly ___
c used for showing that you are annoyed because something has happened later than it should _1_
d someone who has a strong character or is intelligent ___
e extremely large ___
f do something after you have intended to do it for some time ___

In your opinion, is the informal language that Thomas uses appropriate for the meeting? Why? / Why not?

For more on formal and informal language, see Unit 3.

6 🔊50 Listen to the end of the discussion of item 4 on the agenda and complete the sentences with the words and phrases in the box. Do you understand what they mean? Use your dictionary to help you.

reject	seconder	point of order	casting	objections
split	amendment	put the motion	abstentions	

1 Do we accept or _____ the various applications?
2 On a _____ , I'd like to say that I am in favour of considering each application separately.
3 I am happy to accept that proposal unless there are any _____ .
4 OK, so we now have a very concrete proposal from Lisa. Could I have a _____ ? Solange?
5 I now formally _____ to the vote.
6 Any _____ ? No?
7 I'd like to propose a major _____ to the motion before we vote.
8 It's a fifty-fifty _____ .
9 So I am going to use the chairman's _____ vote in favour of the motion.

Further practice

7 🔊51 Pronunciation practice. Practise reading the sentences from 6 aloud. Try to make your speech more formal than usual.

Unit 18 A formal board meeting

Key words
- **application** (noun): a formal request for permission to do or have something
- **authorize** (verb): to give official permission for something to happen
- **motion** (noun): a formal proposal that people discuss and then vote on in a meeting or debate
- **protocol** (noun): a set of rules for the correct way to behave on formal occasions

8 Passives. Complete the sentences using the correct passive form of the verb in brackets. Use the tense information at the end of each sentence to help you. The first one is done for you.
1 The next meeting ___will be held___ (hold) at the head office. (*future will*)
2 At the last meeting the motion _____ (carry). (*past simple*)
3 It _____ (decide) to increase the price by 10%. (*present perfect*)
4 Travel expenses _____ (discuss) before the meeting. (*past perfect*)
5 That _____ (cover) under item 1. (*present simple*)

Over to you

9 In pairs discuss the following statements about formal meetings in English. Do you agree or disagree with them? For each statement, tick the relevant column and give a reason for your opinion.

	Agree	Disagree
1 The language of formal meetings is very old-fashioned.		
2 Formal meetings in English are very well organized.		
3 The language of formal meetings is too complicated.		
4 A lot of people whose first language is English find it difficult to participate fully in formal meetings.		
5 The way in which formal meetings are organized is confusing.		
6 Formal meetings are easy to follow because they always have the same structure.		
7 It is almost impossible for a non-native speaker of English to take part in a formal meeting in English.		

10 Close your book and with a partner brainstorm language used in formal meetings. Write your ideas under these headings. Then look back at the unit and the listening scripts for more ideas.

Opening a formal meeting	Inviting participants to speak	Giving your point of view

11 Now turn to Case study 18 on page 93 for a formal meeting roleplay.

12 For a list of expressions from this unit, see Useful language Unit 18 on page 98.

Unit 19 Writing the minutes

Background

 Toby Training is a small UK-based company which organizes training courses for companies and organizations on a wide range of management issues. One of its one-day courses is on taking minutes of meetings.

Culture point – 'Short and sweet' When some people write, they use very elaborate and complicated language. They also take a long time to produce written texts, because they think they should be pieces of literature. This approach can be a problem when writing minutes of meetings. How would you describe your writing style?

Skills work

1   Read the information about target delegates for the Toby Training course on minute-taking. Then complete the needs analysis sheet below in order to determine your own needs.

Toby Training one-day minute-taking course: Target delegates

- Young inexperienced staff who have never taken minutes before. The focus for these delegates is on developing the skills necessary for taking the minutes of team or progress meetings.
- Middle management who need to take minutes of departmental meetings or even board meetings.
- Very experienced PAs, who may have been taking minutes for years but who want to pick up tips on how to improve their techniques or to be reassured that what they are doing is right!

Minute-Taking Needs Analysis Sheet

What types of meetings do you attend?   Do you take the minutes?   How often?

Tick the problems/difficulties you have when taking minutes in English:

Knowing what information to include in the minutes ☐
Knowing how to lay out the information on the page ☐
Understanding some participants who speak too quickly or not clearly enough ☐
Understanding some specialist or technical language ☐
Writing clear and brief notes of what is being discussed ☐
Deciding on the important points to record in a discussion ☐
Knowing where to sit in the meeting in order to hear and see everybody ☐
Trying to stay awake when the discussion is long and boring! ☐

2   Compare your completed needs analysis sheet with a partner and discuss your requirements.

3   Read what Jack Feldman, a Toby trainer, says about the needs of delegates on his courses. How does your needs analysis compare with what he says? Does anything surprise you?

'People usually have the same needs even though they have different experiences. They nearly all need to learn the skill of taking notes. Many think that minutes need to be a detailed description of who said what, rather than just a list of the topics, decisions and action points. Surprisingly few are aware that it's important to choose carefully where you sit at a meeting to have a good overview of what is happening.'

4   **52** Listen to some participants on a Toby course talking about their experiences and views of minute-taking. What does each person think is the most important thing to do? Write your answers in the table.

Kim Li	Serge Kohler	Laura Bortellotti

5   According to Toby Training, good minutes should answer all of the questions below. Choose the correct words to complete the questions.

   1 What was the date and hour / time of the meeting?
   2 Where was the meeting had / held?
   3 Who attended? And who was not absent / present?
   4 What was / were discussed?
   5 What decisions were achieved / reached?
   6 What action points have / were agreed?
   7 Who was nominated to complete each / every action point?
   8 What deadlines / headlines were agreed?
   9 What handouts, letters and documents were distributed / handed at the meeting?
   10 Are copies of all / every documentation available?
   11 If appropriate, what are the details / information of the next meeting? (date/time/venue/objective)

For more on agendas, see Units 8 and 10.

6   Now read the minutes of a board meeting at Delta International on the next page. Make a note of all the questions in 5 that are answered in these minutes. Which questions are not answered?

Unit 19 Writing the minutes

Minutes of the Delta International Board Meeting

Date/time	24th May 09.00 to 18.00
Venue	Boardroom, Delta International HQ
Minutes of previous meeting	The minutes were agreed unanimously.
Matters arising	The problem concerning the new warehouse was raised by the vice-president.

Topics
1. Price of books and other teaching materials
2. Application for new franchises in the USA (3) and South America (5)
3. Appointment of new MD
4. Office space at HQ

Decisions
1. It was decided to increase the price of all training materials by 5% from the 1st September.
2. All eight new applications for franchises were rejected because of lack of sound financial backing.
3. It was agreed to advertise the post of MD.
4. It was unanimously agreed to rent additional space nearby to extend the HQ accommodation.

Next meeting 28th October at 10.00 at the Hilton Hotel, Heathrow Airport, London

7   Look again at the minutes and answer the questions.
   1. How many of the participants agreed the minutes of the last meeting?
   2. What issue did the vice-president bring up?
   3. Why weren't the new franchise applications successful?
   4. How did they decide to increase the size of the HQ (headquarters)?

Further practice

8   When summarizing the main points of a discussion, it is essential to use a variety of verbs and not just 'say', so that the minutes are not repetitive. Look at the sentences below showing some of these verbs. Then fill in gaps 1–8 with the past simple form of the best verb from the box.

complain   decide   agree   raise   ask   suggest   explain   report

JW ¹_____ holding the next meeting at the airport.
He **brought up** the question of travel expenses.
The chair ²_____ that some action points had not been completed on time.
The marketing director ³_____ on his visit to the IT trade show.
The chairman ⁴_____ his PA to minute the point.
The finance committee **recommended** stopping the project.
It was ⁵_____ to cancel the next meeting.
One point was **discussed** under AOB.
Under any other business she ⁶_____ the question of travel expenses.
The presenter **emphasized** the quality of the product.
The chair ⁷_____ the new procedures.

He **promised** to complete the report by the end of the week.
They all ⁸_____ with the decision.
The team **stressed** their commitment to completing the project on time.

What is the infinitive form of the verbs in bold? And what do those verbs mean? Use your dictionary.

9 🔊 **Pronunciation practice.** Listen to the past simple forms of the verbs from 8 and write them in the correct column of the table according to how many syllables they contain. Then listen again to the two-, three- and four-syllable words and <u>underline</u> the syllable that is stressed. The first word is done for you.

1 syllable	2 syllables	3 syllables	4 syllables
	ag<u>reed</u>		

When you have finished, say all the words aloud with the correct stress.

> **Key words**
> **circulate** (verb): to send something to all the members of a group
> **minute** (verb): to record something in the minutes of a meeting
> **nominate** (verb): to officially suggest that someone should be given a job
> **unanimously** (adverb): (eg agreed) by everyone, without objection

10 These sentences were said by a production manager. Turn them into reported speech using the most appropriate verbs from 8. You may also need to change other words. The first one is done for you.
   1 'Everyone will have an increase in salary next month.' *He promised that everyone would have an increase in salary the following month.*
   2 'I want to say again that I think the quality of this product is excellent.'
   3 'Shall we discuss it under AOB?'
   4 'It is essential to complete the project by next week at the latest.'
   5 'I regret that a lot of colleagues are not fully committed to the project.'

Over to you

11 Prepare your answer to the following question and then discuss it with a partner. Remember to give reasons.

Now that you have almost completed this unit, what in your opinion are the three most important factors to consider when writing minutes? Write your ideas below.
   1 _____
   2 _____
   3 _____

12 Now turn to Case study 19 on page 93 for a practical minute-taking activity.

13 For a list of expressions from this unit, see Useful language Unit 19 on page 98.

Unit 20 Monitoring action and evaluating meetings

Background

In the last unit we looked at the subject of minute-taking via Jack Feldman and his Toby Training course. Now let's move on to another of his courses to focus on the topics of monitoring action points and evaluating performance in meetings.

> *Culture point – 'Can we improve?'* In some cultures there is a tradition of critical evaluation which aims to improve personal performance and procedures. In other cultures criticism can be seen more negatively. What is it like in your country? Are people critical in order to improve things or do they prefer to leave things as they are?

Skills work

1. **54** Listen to Jack talking about the action plan below. Write the dates for each action point in the 'Deadline' column.

   Sample Formal Action Plan

Action point	Responsible person(s)	Deadline	Progress
1 Finish the marketing report	JC		
2 Complete the new sales strategy	JC and PM		
3 Produce the new marketing material	JC and LM		
4 Update the website for the new strategy	Webmaster + team		
5 Organize training course for marketing and sales staff	JC and PM		

2. **55** Now listen to a phone call in which a manager is checking to find out progress on the above action points. Complete the 'Progress' column of the plan in 1 with the letter (a–e) of the correct information below.

   a   About a week late.
   b   Completed before the end of June.
   c   The outline is already complete.
   d   Ready by the deadline on 30th May.
   e   Two weeks ahead of schedule.

3 Look again at Veronica's meeting in Unit 17 and complete the action plan below.

Action point	Responsible person(s)	Deadline
1 Research unusual situations for weddings		
2	Veronica	
3		No date

4 Read this informal action plan. Then complete the sentences below with either 'Formal' or 'Informal'.

> Things to do by next Monday at the latest
> Arrange for the photocopier to be repaired – Sam
> Book a room for the team meeting – Amanda
> Ring TK products to confirm the order – Tania
> Talk to the MD about problems with meeting deadlines – Dom

1 _____ action plans use initials instead of names.
2 _____ action plans set specific dates.
3 _____ action plans are sometimes handwritten.
4 _____ action plans include less important things to do.
5 _____ action plans have first names not full names.
6 _____ action plans are always in electronic form.
7 _____ action plans have clear headings.

For more on different levels of formality, see Units 3 and 18.

5 **56** Now listen to Jack talking about how to monitor action points. Decide whether the sentences are true or false, according to what he says.

1 Most meetings have action points.
2 Action points are never included in the minutes.
3 Action points cannot be monitored in follow-up meetings.
4 A report can be written to show the progress of action points.
5 In some cases a manager may call every day to check on progress of action points.

6 Look at the speech bubbles on the next page, showing how some participants on the Toby course evaluate their performance in meetings. Answer the questions.

Who…
1 …gets worried in meetings?
2 …stops listening when they don't understand?
3 …is the most positive person?
4 …is the most negative person?

My major problem is that I'm not always properly prepared before the meeting. I'm often too busy to read the documents and sometimes I don't even look at the agenda! And at times I get nervous and don't choose the right words and expressions in English, although I usually get there in the end. Also, I don't always listen carefully enough and I sometimes switch off completely if it becomes too difficult.

Karla

I think I am good at observing people's reactions. I always look carefully at people's body language and I try to be aware of how they react when I'm speaking. I also think I am getting better at expressing myself in lively discussions. I am definitely better at letting people finish what they are saying before coming in with my own point.

Moto

I often talk too much and sometimes I can get very argumentative if I feel very strongly about something. I occasionally get aggressive towards people who hold views that I strongly disagree with. And occasionally, I don't ask for explanations or clarification if I don't understand something. Sometimes I find myself agreeing with somebody when I don't really understand.

Sylvie

I think one of my big problems is not maintaining eye contact with other participants when I'm speaking or when they're speaking. But I think I'm getting better at disagreeing diplomatically. And I am much more positive now and try to build bridges if there is conflict.

Clement

7   Which person in 6 do you have most in common with? Are any of them like your colleagues? Discuss with a partner.

8   Write an evaluation of your own performance in recent meetings using the comments in 6 as a model. Work with a partner and share your evaluations. Then report back to the group about each other. Use the following headings as a guide.
- Preparation for the meeting (agenda)
- Relationships with other participants (friendly, relaxed, nervous)
- Confidence when speaking
- Good listener
- Maintaining eye contact / understanding body language

Alinka prepared well for her last meeting. She read the agenda and documents, and thought of some questions to ask...

Further practice

9   **55** Pronunciation practice. Listen again to the conversation in exercise 2 and repeat the lines. Then practise reading the whole dialogue aloud with a partner.

> **Key words**
> **confidence** (noun): the belief that you are able to do things well
> **critical** (adjective): expressing an opinion when you think something is wrong or bad
> **extension** (noun): extra time that you are given to finish a piece of work
> **monitor** (verb): to regularly check something or somebody

10 Make sentences using the comparative or superlative form of the adjectives in brackets. The first one is done for you.
   1 The chairperson's opening words were <u>the most welcoming</u> (welcoming) that I had ever heard.
   2 The production team had _____ (effective) discussion.
   3 The final speaker at the conference gave a _____ (clear) presentation than the other presenters.
   4 The monitoring of the action points after the meeting was _____ (detailed) than usual.
   5 Her preparation for the meeting was _____ (bad) we had ever seen.
   6 He wrote _____ (good) report.
   7 Well, that's taking a bit _____ (long) than we thought.
   8 She is _____ (positive) person in the team.

Over to you

11 Prepare an answer to this question and then discuss it with a partner.

What are the positive and negative effects of evaluating your own performance? Draw a table like the one below, and write your ideas under the two headings: 'Positive effects' and 'Negative effects'.

Positive effects	Negative effects

12 In groups, plan and enact a start-to-finish roleplay of a meeting, incorporating ideas and techniques that you have learnt from all the units in the book. Make sure you:
   • agree who you are and what the meeting is about
   • decide on the items on the agenda
   • choose a chair for the meeting
   • have the chair open the meeting
   • nominate participants to prepare specific items on the agenda
   • plan who is going to agree, disagree or make other suggestions
   • finish the meeting appropriately, including a summary by the chair.

13 Now turn to Case study 20 on page 93 for a further activity in evaluating your own performance.

14 For a list of expressions from this unit, see Useful language Unit 20 on page 98.

Case studies

Case study 1

Imagine you are a trainer for a management training company. Prepare a short presentation on different types of meetings using the definitions in exercise 5 on page 8 as a model. You could design a PowerPoint slide or similar to support your presentation, if you have the software.

Then make the presentation in front of an audience. How did it go?

Case study 2

Work in pairs. Decide who is student A and who is student B. Then read through your specific instructions below before starting the roleplay.

Student A: You are Sandy Smart. You work for a pharmaceutical company and want to arrange a meeting with Dr Miller, the senior partner at a medical centre, in order to present some of your new products. Phone Dr Miller and arrange a time to meet next week for about half an hour. This is your schedule for next week:

Monday
Team meeting 09.00 to 10.30
Presentation (Dr Adams) 18.00 to 18.30
Tuesday
Working from home (finish report) until 13.00
Office in the afternoon (videoconference 15.30 to 16.00)
Wednesday
Staff training day (Wedge Hall 8.30 to 18.30 followed by dinner)
Thursday
Presentation (Stoke Health Centre) 10.30 to 11.00
Office (interviews for new representative job) 14.00 to 17.00
Friday
Meeting with marketing manager 09.00 to 10.00
Dentist 11.00 to 12.00

Student B: You are Dr Miller, the senior partner at a medical centre. You receive a phone call from Sandy Smart, a representative from a pharmaceutical company, who wants to arrange a meeting for about half an hour in order to present some of the company's new products. You are very busy but you try to find a suitable time. This is your schedule for next week:

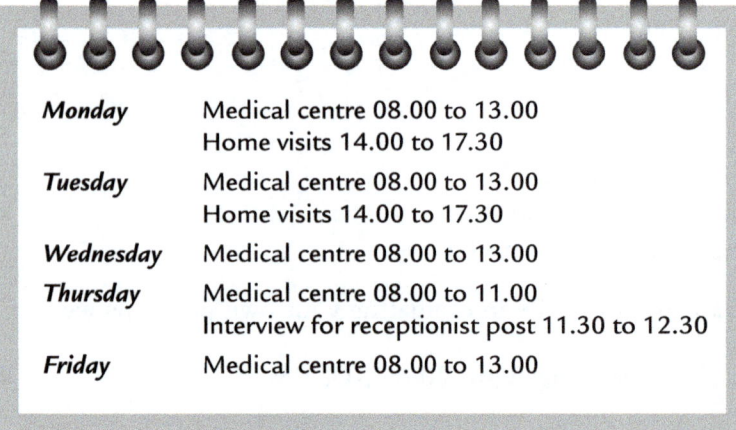

Monday   Medical centre 08.00 to 13.00
                Home visits 14.00 to 17.30
Tuesday   Medical centre 08.00 to 13.00
                Home visits 14.00 to 17.30
Wednesday   Medical centre 08.00 to 13.00
Thursday   Medical centre 08.00 to 11.00
                Interview for receptionist post 11.30 to 12.30
Friday   Medical centre 08.00 to 13.00

Case study 3

Write an email to a client, customer, supplier or colleague about a meeting you are organizing next month. Decide whether the email should be formal or informal and use suitable language. Include some of the following ideas if you wish:

- mention a phone call you have just had
- refer to an attachment that you are sending with the email
- confirm the time and date of the next meeting
- talk about an aspect of the project that you have just finished
- refer to some work you need to complete.

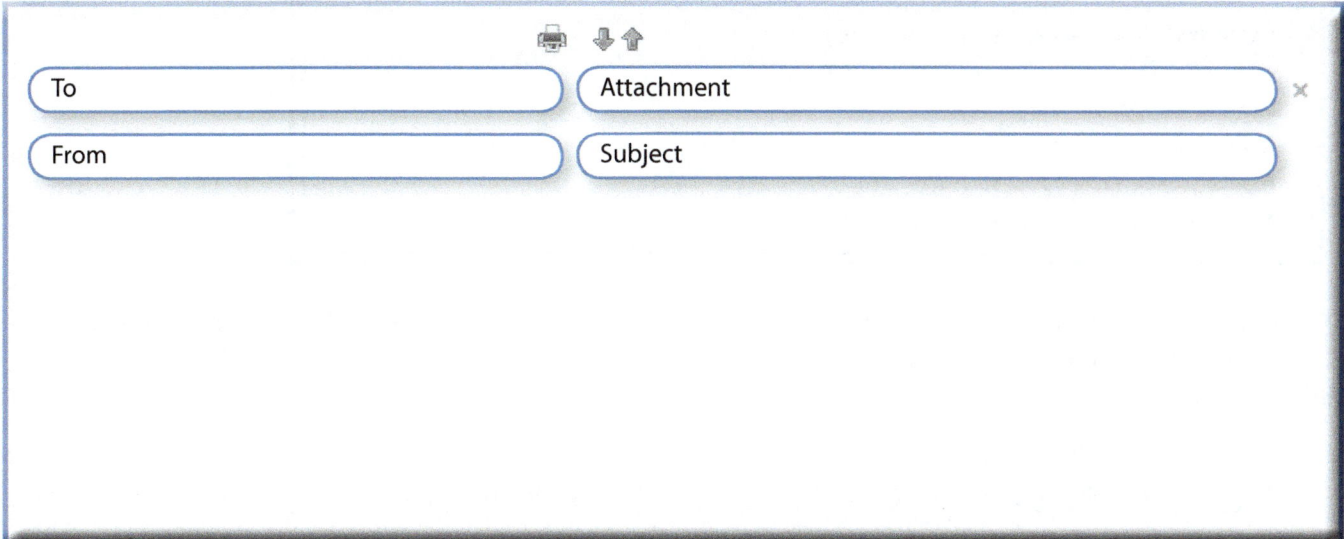

Case study 4

Write one of the following emails:
- an email to cancel a brainstorming meeting about the company logo
- an email to postpone a meeting to discuss the new company marketing brochure.

Use the new language from the unit and make sure that you give a good reason for cancelling or postponing.

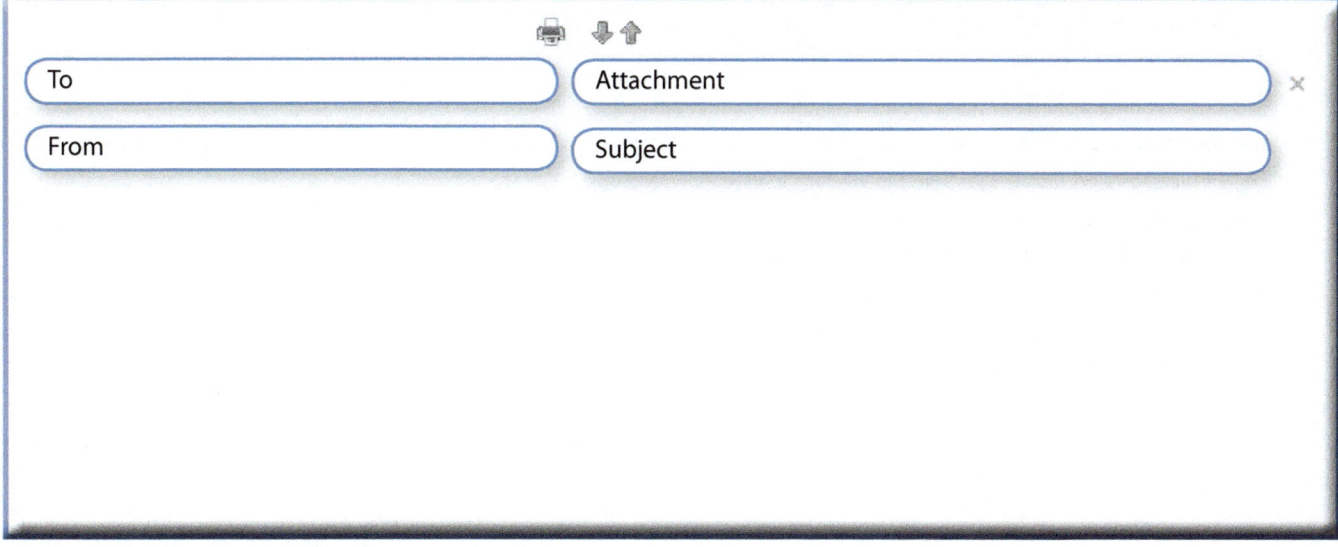

Then make a phone call for the other situation.

Case study 5

Work in pairs. Decide who is student A and who is student B. Then read through your specific instructions below before starting the roleplay.

Student A: You are Jack Dando from Transit Publishers. You want to book accommodation in a business centre. Ring the centre and try to make a booking for the following meeting:

> **Meeting:** Sales conference
> **Dates:** 1 day in the week beginning 4th December
> **Accommodation:** 1 large conference room (60 people), 5 meeting rooms (12 people each)
> **Equipment:** Multimedia projector and interactive whiteboard (in conference room), wireless Internet and flip charts (in meeting rooms)
> **General equipment:** Photocopier
> **Refreshments:** Drinks machine
> **Meals:** Lunch from 13.00 to 14.00
> **Price:** Ask the price and try to get a reduction

Student B: You are Henrietta Morita from the Capital Conference Centre. You receive a phone call from Jack Dando, who wants to book accommodation for a large meeting. Answer his/her questions with the following information:

Available dates: 6th and 8th December
Accommodation:
You have three large conference rooms:
- Conference room 1 (seats 120 people)
- Conference room 2 (seats 80 people)
- Conference room 3 (seats 50 people)

You have 10 meeting rooms:
- 3 rooms for 12 people
- 2 rooms for 16 people
- 5 rooms for 20 people

Equipment: All conference rooms have multimedia projectors and interactive whiteboards, all meeting rooms have Wi-Fi, laptops and flip charts. Technician always available for support
General equipment: Photocopier in the resource centre
Refreshments: No drinks machine – drinks and light refreshments are served in the rooms at agreed times
Meals: We can serve lunch in the restaurant at an agreed time – a varied menu
Price: $120 per delegate, including lunch and other refreshments
Reduction: Offer a 5% reduction. If Jack Dando is not happy with the reduction, offer a final discount of 10%

Case study 6

Think of a real or imaginary meeting you are arranging. Write the details of the meeting in the table. Use some of the following ideas if you wish:
- Type of meeting: brainstorming, progress, project, appraisal, training
- Venue: your office, company seminar room, meeting room in hotel, training centre
- Subject: salaries and expenses, company logo, move to new office accommodation

Subject	
Date and time	
Venue	
Participants	

Then work with a partner and answer the following questions about the meeting:
1. Is the meeting really necessary or could everything be done by email, phone or videoconference?
2. Would it be better if mini-groups met to discuss specific points before the meeting?
3. What do you want to achieve in the meeting?
4. Is it a formal or informal meeting?
5. Who are the most important attendees in order to achieve the aims of the meeting?
6. Have you chosen the best date and time?
7. Is the venue appropriate?
8. What facilities and equipment are needed?

Case study 7

Imagine you are at a big international meeting for a global electronics company, taking place in Los Angeles, USA, and you need to make small talk with the other delegates. Choose two of the following characters to play the part of:
- Christine Evans, a PA from the Los Angeles office
- Hiroshi Sato, a programmer from the Tokyo office
- Irena Fernández Sánchez, a marketing executive from the Madrid office
- Lazlo Varga, a sales manager from the Budapest office
- Michael Graves, a director from the London office

Work with different partners, using the ideas in the speech bubbles to make small talk. Try to be as amusing/inventive/creative as possible in your answers and to talk for one minute with each person – then change partners. If the person you are speaking to has chosen the same character as you, play the part of your second choice instead.

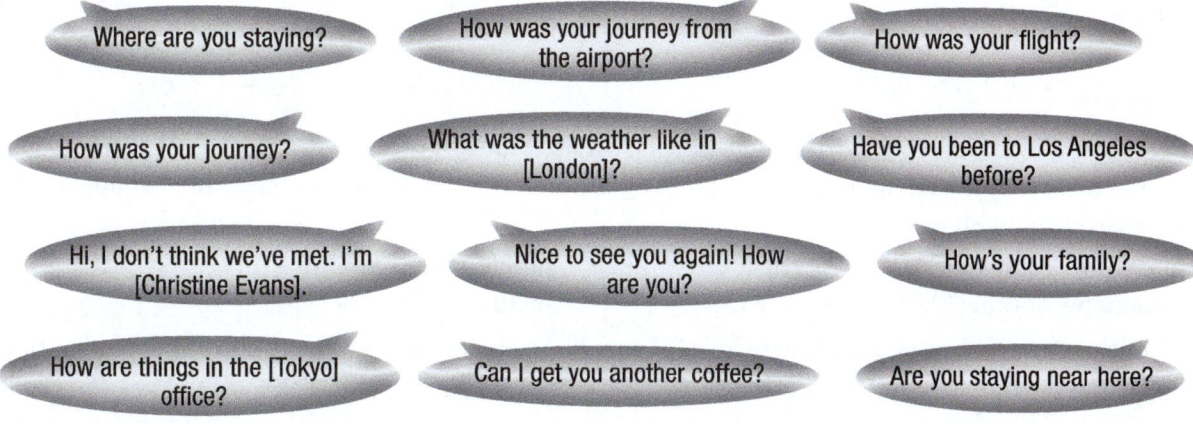

Case study 8

You are Alison Spear, the new Managing Director of Solent Pleasure, a company which sells luxury yachts. This is your first opportunity to meet with the sales and marketing teams, and you need to get the meeting started. Follow the instructions below, remembering to allow a suitable amount of time between instructions 5 and 6.

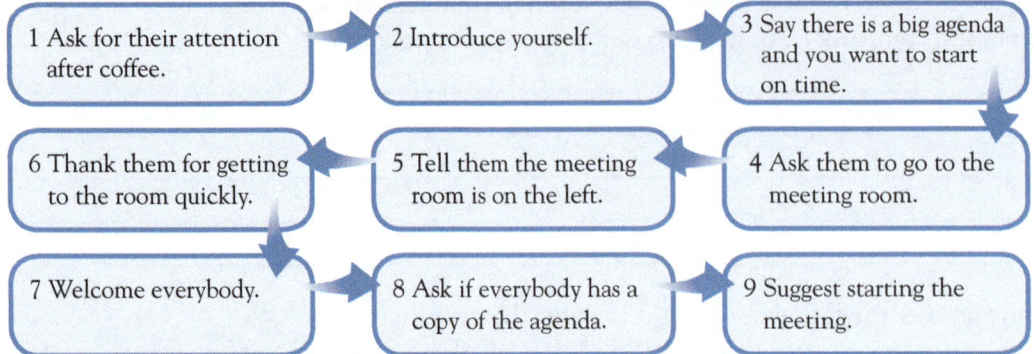

1 Ask for their attention after coffee.
2 Introduce yourself.
3 Say there is a big agenda and you want to start on time.
4 Ask them to go to the meeting room.
5 Tell them the meeting room is on the left.
6 Thank them for getting to the room quickly.
7 Welcome everybody.
8 Ask if everybody has a copy of the agenda.
9 Suggest starting the meeting.

Case study 9

Look at the photographs. How might these people introduce themselves at a meeting? Imagine you are one of them and introduce yourself – can your partner guess which person you are? Do the same for all the photos.

Case study 10

Imagine you are chairing the Monday morning team meeting in your company. Look at the agenda and your notes. Briefly introduce the agenda to give an overview of what the meeting is going to be about.

Item 1 Welcome	— Introduce and welcome a new member to the team (Mamdouh Mohammed / engineer / IT expert / worked before in a similar company in US)
Item 2 Report on quarterly sales figures	— Sales were 20% up last quarter
Item 3 Redecoration of offices	— Offices will be painted in August, with new carpets and office furniture. Need to empty desks and filing cabinets before holidays
Item 4 Visit from CEO	— Diane Lowe (new CEO) will visit on 10th May
AOB	

Case study 11

You are chairing a videoconference with three people: Silvie (France), Gerd (Germany) and Gianni (Italy). You want to check that the equipment is working properly. Practise the discussion orally in a group. Use the following ideas if you wish:

- equipment working OK?
- microphone working OK?
- hear OK?
- see OK?
- problems with sound?
- picture quality OK?

Members of the group can use the following ideas of possible problems to answer the chairperson's questions:

- picture dark/distorted/crystal clear/OK/fine
- sound crackly/faint/OK

Case study 12

Work in groups of four, taking it in turns to be the chairperson. Choose one of the following topics to discuss. The role of the participants in the meeting is to disrupt the discussion as much as possible; it is your job to keep it on track. It might be best if you prepare your chosen topic as a homework assignment before you do it in class.

- A tour of the new warehouse
- A planned visit to a trade fair
- Travel expenses
- The new photocopier
- The newly installed computer network

See the Useful language section for appropriate phrases for keeping people on the topic.

Case study 13

Work in pairs. Decide who is student A and who is student B. Then read through your specific instructions below before starting the roleplay.

Student A: You are the manager of a small company and because of a big drop in profits you have to fire a member of your staff. Choose one of the people below to fire, and justify your reasons to student B (the deputy manager). Try to be as diplomatic as possible.

Student B: You are the deputy manager of a small company where there has been a drop in profits. The manager (student A) is going to suggest one of the people below to fire, and you disagree strongly with the decision. Justify your reasons in a discussion with student A.

A: I think we should fire…because…   B: I disagree completely…

Name: Mandy Johansson	Name: Bill Roberts	Name: Roy Batchford	Name: Laura Ruggiero
Age: 35	Age: 55	Age: 23	Age: 40
Family: Single mother, two children	Family: Wife and three children	Family: Single	Family: Single but looks after elderly mother
Job: Accountant	Job: Sales representative	Job: Trainee sales representative	Job: Market researcher
Time with company: 3 years	Time with company: 14 years	Time with company: 6 months	Time with company: 5 years
Salary: $45,000	Salary: $60,000	Salary: $20,000	Salary: $44,000
Appraisal: Good worker and a skilled accountant, but often has time off to look after children.	Appraisal: His performance has dropped. His wife has been ill for some time. Was our best sales rep.	Appraisal: Very dynamic, lots of fresh ideas. But a newcomer to the company, so still much to learn.	Appraisal: Good worker, but has been late for work on several occasions over recent months.

Case study 14

Work with a partner. Take it in turns to break the following bad news. Then follow the instructions below to evaluate how you did.

1. Your partner had an interview for an internal promotion the previous week, for the post of area sales manager. Tell him/her that the post has been offered to a younger colleague.
2. Your partner has asked for a week's additional leave because of minor illness in his family. Tell him/her that there is too much work on at the moment and unfortunately it is not possible to agree to the request.
3. Your partner asked for a pay rise. Tell him/her that the request has been refused because the company is currently making a loss.
4. Tell your partner that you are not completely happy with the quality of his/her work. Say that this is the first official warning and that if there is not sufficient improvement it could result in him/her being fired.

After the roleplays evaluate how effectively you each broke the bad news:

- Was the manager sympathetic?
- Was the message too direct?
- Did the manager try to 'soften' the bad news?
- Did the manager upset you?

Then give the manager a score between 1 (poor) and 10 (excellent) for his/her performance.

Case study 15

Work in groups. Have brainstorming meetings on the following topics:
1. The most suitable Christmas present for a valued customer.
2. The best place in your continent to hold an international sales conference.
3. What the cover for a new textbook on strategic management should look like.
4. A new product to introduce into the soft drinks market.

Try to use as many expressions from the unit as possible during the brainstorm.

Case study 16

Work in pairs. Decide who is student A and who is student B. Then read through your specific instructions below before starting the roleplay.

Student A: You are a management consultant. You have just completed some work for a client in which their office layout has been restructured in order to make communication more effective. Present your proposals and answer the client's questions. You suggest the following:
- remove all existing walls and create a completely open-plan office
- arrange workstations in groups of four or six and ensure that people who work together sit near to each other
- create lots of space around groups of workstations to prevent workers feeling boxed in
- arrange for storage space to be next to teams
- have two enclosed offices for interviews and meetings.

Student B: You are the owner of a small company and you have asked a consultant to redesign your main office in order to improve communication within teams. Listen to what the consultant tells you and then ask the following questions:
- How much will it cost to remove all the walls?
- Will an open-plan office be noisy?
- How much storage space will each team be able to have?
- Will the managers have offices?
- Which rooms will be enclosed?

Case study 17

Discuss with a partner the most common problems which occur at the end of a meeting. Use some of the following ideas if you wish:
- Participants are tired and are not concentrating.
- The meeting is just before lunch and participants are hungry.
- There has been a lot of disagreement and participants are in a bad mood.
- The meeting has gone on too long because it was badly chaired.
- One of the main items was a presentation which was long and boring.
- The chairperson is irritated and in a bad mood.
- The meeting has not achieved its objective.

Case study 18

Work in groups to plan and perform a formal meeting. You all work for a newly started IT company and are meeting to decide about your new office. You must decide on the following:
- the location of the premises
- the size of the head office
- the facilities in the office
- whether to hire or purchase cars for the sales representatives.

Try to use as much of the new language from the unit as possible during the meeting.

Case study 19

Use the Toby Training template below to write the minutes of the last meeting you attended. Alternatively, choose a meeting from one of the units in the book, for example Unit 10 or Unit 15.

Template for Writing Minutes

It is important for minutes to have clear headings for the different parts of the meeting, so that people can quickly access key information. The following headings are suitable for most meetings (except informal).

Minutes of the _____ meeting
Date/time
Venue
Present
Apologies
Minutes of previous meeting

Documents/handouts
Matters arising
Topics
Decisions
Action points (responsible/deadline)
Next meeting (date/time/venue/objective)

Case study 20

Look at Toby Training's chair evaluation checklist. Think about the last time you chaired a meeting and tick all the things in the list that you did. Add up the number of ticks and then check your score with the key below. Compare your answers with your colleagues. How good a chairperson are you?

(If you haven't chaired a meeting yet, hold on to this checklist for now and then complete it immediately after your first meeting as chairperson.)

Chair evaluation checklist

1. I welcomed the participants warmly.
2. I made participants feel at home.
3. I introduced the participants to each other.
4. I clarified the objectives of the meeting.
5. I established the ground rules.
6. I dealt with all organizational matters.
7. I managed the discussion effectively.
8. I stuck to the agenda and timings.
9. I dealt with questions fairly.
10. I always checked that the participants understood.
11. I managed voting procedures effectively.
12. I summarized discussions clearly.
13. I clarified action points.
14. I checked to see if there were AOB items.
15. I set the date of the next meeting.

Key
Number of boxes ticked:
0 to 4   Go back to the drawing board!
5 to 9   Go on a Toby Training course!
10 to 13 Ask for a promotion, an increase in salary, or both!
14 or 15 You are a star! Congratulations!

Useful language

Unit 1

Types of meeting

I'm just calling about organizing a **videoconference**.
Is it possible to discuss the new logo at our next **team meeting**?
I was ringing to try and fix up the next **progress meeting**.
I was thinking of setting up a **brainstorming meeting**.
We need to decide on the date of the **AGM**.
Can we fix a date for your **annual appraisal**?
I'd like to organize a **training day** on the new software.

Unit 2

Asking to meet

Could we find a time to meet?
Can we arrange to meet sometime?
Can you organize a conference call?
Any chance *(informal)* of a meeting this week?
Could we try to arrange a meeting before Friday?
What about Monday morning?
How about after lunch at, say, two o'clock?
I'd like to schedule a meeting before the end of the month. Can you suggest a few dates?
Can we try and agree on a day in the middle of the month?

Responding to a meeting request

Yes, I can make that date.
Yes, I'm free on that date.
Tuesday at nine is fine for me.
Wednesday 15th sounds good.
Yes, that date works for me.
Sorry, I can't make next Wednesday.
I'm afraid I have another appointment then.
I can't. I'm away on a business trip.

Unit 3

Formal email language

Dear colleagues/Ms Tidman/Mr Timm,
I trust you are all well.
I look forward to meeting/seeing you on the 15th July.
I detail below…
I would advise…
As discussed,…
Please find herewith…
Please find attached…
Yours sincerely,
Best wishes/regards, *(can also be informal depending on the context)*

Informal/friendly email language

Hello Uwe/Hi Jenny/Dear Paul,
It was good to speak the other day.
Sorry for the (long) delay.
I've attached…
I'm looking forward to our meeting.
See you on Thursday.
All the best,
Cheers,

Unit 4

Confirming arrangements

So we're meeting on Thursday at nine. Is that right?
Let me make a note of the date and the time.
Can I check the details of the meeting with you again?
So I'll see you on Wednesday at four o'clock in your office, OK?
So we've decided to meet on the 7th of May then?
I'm looking forward to seeing you on the 5th at 10am.

Rescheduling and cancelling meetings

I'm afraid I'm going to have to ask you if we can reschedule our meeting.
Something has come up and I can't get out of it. *(informal)*
Have you got another date in mind?
Is there any chance *(informal)* of postponing the meeting until the following week?
Could we go for *(informal)* the same day and the same time?
Sorry about this, but it really couldn't be helped.
I'm afraid that I'm going to have to postpone our meeting till later in the month.
The problem has now been solved, so we have cancelled the meeting.

Unit 5

Booking rooms at a business centre

I'm ringing about booking the centre for a management training course.
Can I check your availability before I go into detail about facilities?
What date did you have in mind? – Well ideally, we

are looking at June 13th.
Can you just go through what you could offer us? – Well, we've got four main seminar rooms. The floor plan is on our website.

Talking about facilities

We have multimedia projectors, interactive whiteboards, wireless Internet, TV, video, DVD and laptops.
How are the rooms laid out? – You can have whatever layout you like.
What arrangements are there for refreshments? –
We can serve refreshments in the training rooms or in the restaurant.
And car parking? – We have free car parking for up to 70 cars.

Unit 6

Getting participants involved

Can we start with you, Jerry?
So who'd like to go next?
OK, so who's going to go next?
Can we bring you in now, Paul?

Saying that something is important

It's essential to…
It's important to…
It's vital to…
It's crucial to…

Commenting positively on what people say

That's really/extremely interesting.
That was very useful.
You've made some very good points.

Unit 7

In reception before a meeting

I'm here for the AquaTec meeting.
Let me just check your name off on the list.
Here are the additional papers for the meeting.
Here's your name badge.
Where can I leave my coat/bag?
You can leave your coat/bag here in reception.
Where do I go now?
Coffee is being served in the Green Room.
The lift is over there.

Introductions and greetings

Hello, I don't think we've met before. My name's…
Let me introduce you to…
This is…He's/She's the marketing manager / in the production team.
Nice/Pleased to meet you.
Have you met…? – Yes, we already know each other. / No, I don't think we have.
How are you? – Very well, thank you. And you? – Fine thanks.

Small talk

How was your flight? – Terrible! We were delayed three hours.
Did you get a taxi from the airport? – Yes, it was really quick. There was no traffic.
Are you staying near here? – Yes, at the Hilton.
Can I get you another coffee? – Yes please, that's kind of you.
What was the weather like when you left New York? – Really hot! Much warmer than here.

Unit 8

Attracting people's attention

Dear colleagues! Sorry to interrupt your fun, but could I have your attention please?
We have a lot to discuss.
I think it's time we made a start.

Opening a meeting

I think we can launch proceedings now.
Let's get the ball rolling. (informal)
Let's get this show on the road! (very informal)
Let me introduce myself formally to everybody. I'm…
I'm chairing the meeting and my PA is taking the minutes.
Does everyone have a copy of the agenda?
Well, to start with, just a few formalities and some organizational matters.
Renate Bromma, our finance director, has sent her apologies. She's snowed under (informal) with the quarterly sales figures.
We're aiming to work through till one.
We plan to finish at three-ish. (informal)

Unit 9

The chair's comments about introductions

I think it would be good to start the meeting with a few introductions.
It's the quickest way of getting to know each other.
Could you all say a few things about yourselves and what you are doing at the moment?
I'll start off and we'll go clockwise/anti-clockwise round the table after that.
Well, that's me in a nutshell. (*informal*)
So now it's over to you! Would you like to start?
Could you focus on just the main facts, please?
We need to make sure we have enough time for everybody.

Introducing yourself

I was born in…
I went to school in…and after school I studied…
I got a degree in…
I worked for a year as a…in…
My first job was as a…
Two years ago, I got a job as a…
About five years ago I joined…
Last year I was offered a job as…
I started my current job…months ago.
I've been working for/at…for three years.

Unit 10

Clarifying the agenda

I'd like to say a few words about the agenda.
The aim of this meeting is…
Can I ask you to look at the agenda?
Under item 2 I'd like to talk about…
After that, under item 3 we need to focus on…
Fourthly, I will clarify salary and expenses.
Following that, the fifth item is to decide who does what and when.
Then finally, under any other business I'd like to mention a new development.

Opening items on the agenda

OK then, let me talk you through item two.
Can we move on to the next item?
Let's turn to the next item.
OK, so that brings us to the next item.
So, shall we turn to item three?
Let's take up the topic of…
That brings us finally to any other business.

Closing items on the agenda

Does anyone have any further questions at this point?
I think that ties up that topic.
That covers that item.
Well, I think that's all we need to say about that issue.
Well, I think that resolves that issue.
So, any more questions at this point?

Unit 11

Checking the equipment

Can I check a few technical details?
Is your equipment/microphone working OK?
Can you all hear/see me?
Is anybody having problems with the sound or picture quality?

Commenting about the equipment

The picture is very dark/a bit distorted/fine.
The sound is a bit faint but I can see you clearly.
The sound is crystal clear/a bit crackly.

Setting the ground rules

Could I ask you all not to interrupt when someone else is talking?
If you want to speak, can you raise a hand?
Could you speak one at a time?
Could you make your disagreement positive?
Don't just say that something is rubbish (*informal*) – suggest an alternative.

Unit 12

Expressing opinions

I think/don't think that…
I don't know how you feel but I think…
As I see it,…
In my opinion,…
Well personally, I think…
If you ask me (*informal*), I think…

Making suggestions and recommendations

Can I make a suggestion?
I suggest keeping the Tara logo.
How about changing the colour?
I'd like to suggest we keep the old logo.
Let me make a recommendation.
I recommend we change the colour of the logo.
That's my recommendation.

Keeping people on the topic
Let's not go into that now.
We'll come to that later on.
I don't want to get sidetracked.
Can we discuss that later, please?
I don't want to get off the point.
Let's stick to the topic, please.

Unit 13
Focusing attention on a topic
We all know why we are having this meeting today.
So straight to the point. (informal)
Let's not waste any time. (informal)
And we must start today.
There's no time to waste. (informal)

Agreeing and disagreeing
I agree with you entirely.
I couldn't agree with you more.
I disagree completely with that.
I'm completely against that.
I'm not convinced by your argument.
Don't get me wrong (informal),…but…

Unit 14
Encouraging people to be positive and 'softening' language
Shall we try and focus on the positive points?
Looking at this positively, you've already achieved your main objective.
You can look at it in two ways.
Unfortunately,…
I'm sorry to say/tell you that…
It's with great regret that…

Bringing people into the conversation
Can I get some reaction from you now?
Would you like to start, Andrew?
Could I ask you to come in now, Tony?
What do you think?
What are your thoughts?

Unit 15
Clarifying and summarizing
So to clarify, we need to highlight the wide range of services.
I'll just clarify again what we've come up with so far.
I'll go over that again to make sure it's clear.
I'll say the main points again to be sure they're clear.
Here's what we've come up with so far.
I'll just run through what we've suggested so far.
I'll just go through what we have suggested.
Let me run through what we've agreed.
OK, let's summarize what we've been saying.
I think we've come up with several major areas. Firstly,…
I'll just summarize what has been suggested.

Commenting on other people's ideas
I think it sounds too clinical.
I think Sheila has a good point.
I'd like to come in here.
I agree completely with Tom.
I'm really not convinced by that argument.
That's really not how I see it.

Unit 16
Inviting questions
I welcome your feedback.
Please feel free to ask me questions at any time.
Any questions so far?

Going over things again and asking for clarification
Can I just ask you to run through that again, please?
Could you tell us a little bit more about that?
Let me put it another way.
In other words,…
Is that clear to everybody?
What I'm trying to say is that…
Does that clarify things?
Have I made that clear enough? – That's very clear.

Unit 17
Doing a summary
I think it's best if I just run through the main points we've agreed.
It's always better to summarize decisions formally.
I think we've come up with three projects.
Firstly, we've agreed that we'll make a 30 minute documentary.

Confirming action and deadlines
I will get back to you by the end of January.
So you'll check that by what date?
I should be able to give you an answer by Friday.
So you'll do the research by the end of the month?

Useful language

Confirming what has been discussed or decided

We've decided to produce three documentaries.
I think that covers the main points that have been decided.
I confirm that we want to make a film.
It seems that we are all decided to make a documentary.
Just to confirm, the documentary will be 30 minutes long.

Unit 18

Opening a formal meeting

I'm delighted to see so many of you present.
It is crucial that we have a quorum today.
Firstly, a few administrative matters.
We have apologies from Tony Jefferson.
They have authorized two other colleagues to make their proxy votes.
Can I sign the minutes of the last meeting as a correct record?
Are there any items arising from the minutes?
I can report that all action points have been carried out within the required deadlines.

Inviting participants to speak

Who would like to start?
Could we hear the Italian perspective from you?
Who else would like to come in at this point?
Maybe you'd like to come in now?
Would you like to say a few words?

Voting

Do we accept or reject the various applications?
I propose we vote on each set of applications separately. Is that accepted?
On a point of order, I'd like to say that I am in favour of the motion.
Are there any objections?
We now have a very concrete proposal.
Could I have a seconder for the proposal?
I'm happy to second the proposal.
I second the motion.
The motion is that we accept the franchise applications from Hong Kong.
I now formally put the motion to the vote.
Raise your hands if you are in favour/against the motion.
Any abstentions?
I hereby declare that the motion was carried.
The vote was unanimous.
It's a 50-50 split, so I am going to use the chairman's casting vote in favour of the motion.

Unit 19

Verbs to write in the minutes instead of 'said'

They all **agreed** with the decision.
The chairman **asked** his PA to minute the point.
He **brought up** the question of expenses.
The chair **complained** that some action points had not been completed.
It was **decided** to cancel the meeting.
One point was **discussed** under AOB.
The presenter **emphasized** the quality of the product.
The chair **explained** the procedures.
He **promised** to complete the report.
Under AOB she **raised** the question of expenses.
He **recommended** stopping the project.
The marketing director **reported** on his visit to the trade show.
The team **stressed** their commitment to the project.
JW **suggested** holding the next meeting at the airport.

Unit 20

Checking and reporting on progress

I was just wondering how things were progressing with the action points?
How is the report progressing?
Is that finished yet?
Two weeks ahead of schedule.
It will be finished/ready by the end of next week/the deadline on 30th May.
That's taking a bit longer than we thought.
Don't worry,... (*informal*)
The website is a bit behind schedule.
I don't think we'll make the deadline.
I think we'll be about a week late in finishing that.
No problem there. (*informal*)

Listening scripts

Unit 1

1

1
Barbara Koenig: Delta International. Barbara Koenig speaking.
Rick Casbon: Good morning, Barbara. It's Rick Casbon here. Can I speak to Uwe Timm, please?
BK: Good morning, Mr Casbon. Mr Timm is in his office. I'll put you straight through.
Uwe Timm: Uwe Timm.
RC: Good morning, Uwe. It's Rick here.
UT: Hello Rick. How are you?
RC: Fine. I'm just calling about organizing a videoconference for the board…

2
Tom Buddell: Hello Paul. Tom here.
Paul Hoffman: Oh hi Tom, I didn't think you'd be in the office today.
TB: Yeah, I was meant to be going to the printers, but it was cancelled at the last minute. Paul, I just wanted to ask something. Is it possible to discuss the new logo for IGP Products at our next team meeting?
PH: Sure.

3
Paul Hoffman: Paul Hoffman speaking. How can I help?
Jenny Tidman: Hi Paul. Jenny Tidman here.
PH: Oh hi Jenny. How are you?
JT: Fine. Well, OK, just a bit on the busy side. Do you have a minute to spare, Paul?
PH: Yeah sure, fire away.
JT: Well, I was ringing to try and fix up the next progress meeting with the design team for the Business Spanish book project…

4
Jenny Tidman: Delta International. Jenny Tidman speaking.
Uwe Timm: Hi Jenny. It's Uwe here. Have you got time to talk?
JT: Yeah sure.
UT: I was thinking of setting up a meeting to brainstorm ideas for improving the website.
JT: That sounds like a good idea.

5
Uwe Timm: Hello Rick. It's Uwe here. Sorry for ringing so early!
Rick Casbon: No problem. What can I do for you?
UT: Well, we really need to decide on the final date of the annual general meeting. I'm finalizing the company calendar this week.

6
Jenny Tidman: Good morning. Jenny Tidman speaking.
Uwe Timm: Morning Jenny. Uwe here. Do you think we could possibly fix a date and a time for your annual appraisal? I'd like to do it before the end of the month if possible. Can you suggest a few dates?

7
Paul Hoffman: Paul Hoffman.
Jenny Tidman: Morning Paul.
PH: Oh hi, Jenny. How are you?
JT: Fine thanks. Paul, do you remember we spoke about organizing a training day using that new software? Well, the company that produces it has agreed to send one of their top engineers down to spend a day with the team in July.
PH: Great!

2
(see unit for the sentences)

Unit 2

3

1
Jenny: Paul, can we try and agree on a day in the middle of July for the staff development meeting?
Paul: Sure. I think the 15th or the 16th would be perfect.
Jenny: Great. Let's go for the 15th then. Can you…

2
Uwe: Rick, I would like to include the date of the AGM in the company calendar. Can we agree the final date now?
Rick: Yes, sure. If I recall correctly we opted for the second or third week in November?
Uwe: Yes, that's right. The 12th or the 19th. Do you have a preference?
Rick: Not really, no.
Uwe: Shall we settle for the 12th then?
Rick: Yeah, that's fine by me. Whatever date we choose will be good for some and problematic for others…

3
Paul: Paul Hoffman.
Uwe: Hi Paul. Can I come and meet you and the team this week? I'd like to talk about some new projects.
Paul: Sure, Uwe. Well, we have our regular team meeting on Thursday morning. Would you like to come to that?
Uwe: Sounds perfect.
Paul: We normally meet from 9.30 to 10.30. Is that OK?
Uwe: Yeah, that's great. Thanks.

4
Uwe: Hi Jenny. As you know, I'd like to set up a brainstorming meeting about the new website. I thought of involving you, Paul and myself initially.
Jenny: Fine. When did you have in mind?
Uwe: What about Wednesday afternoon? Say, three o'clock? Is that OK for you?
Jenny: Let me just have a look. No, I'm tied up then in another meeting. I could make four o'clock though.
Uwe: OK. Let's go for that. That will work for Paul. He's already told me when he's free…

5
Rick: Uwe, can you organize a videoconference with at least three or four of the board members sometime on Friday? It's quite urgent.
Uwe: That's quite short notice!
Rick: Yes I know, but we must have the meeting before the weekend.
Uwe: OK. Well, I'll see what I can do. Shall I try and fix it for 3pm GMT again?
Rick: That would be great.
Uwe: OK, I'll get back to you later today to confirm.
Rick: Thanks very much, Uwe. You're a star!

6
Uwe: Hi Jenny, it's about your annual appraisal. Can we fix a date before the end of the month?
Jenny: I'm sorry Uwe, but I really can't do anything this month. I'm completely tied up. How about the very beginning of next month? Say, the 1st or the 2nd?
Uwe: The 2nd would be good for me. What about an early morning meeting?
Jenny: That's fine by me. Say, seven o'clock?
Uwe: Yeah, great. Thursday 2nd April. I'll…

4
(see answer key for the sentences)

5
A: Can we arrange to meet sometime?
B: Yes, sure. How about Thursday or Friday?
A: I'm tied up at the end of the week. What about next Monday?
B: That would be OK for me. Shall we say after lunch at about two?
A: I'd prefer Monday morning actually.
B: OK. Monday morning at ten?

Unit 3

6
(see unit for the email addresses)

Unit 4

7
(see unit for the dialogues)

Unit 5

8
Receptionist: Century Business Centre. How can I help?
Emily: Good morning. My name's Emily Maitland, from ArrowInsurance. I'm ringing about booking the centre for a management training course on organizing meetings.
Receptionist: Yes, certainly.
Emily: Can I first check your availability before I go into detail about facilities?
Receptionist: Yes, of course. What date did you have in mind?

Emily: Well ideally, we are looking at June 13th.
Receptionist: Would you need the whole centre? Or just a selection of rooms?
Emily: Well, there'll be about 30 delegates, and we'd need a room for all 30 at the start and end of the day…and then we'd like to split them into four or five groups for the rest of the time.
Receptionist: Well, at the moment another company has made a provisional booking for our presentation theatre that day, but all of the other rooms are available. So I think that would suit your needs.
Emily: OK, can you just go through what you could offer us?
Receptionist: Well, we've got four main seminar rooms. The biggest holds 48 people, so that would be ideal for your large group meeting. The others hold 36, 16 and eight. I think there would be plenty of space for splitting the delegates up for group tasks. The floor plan is on our website, so you can easily check for yourself.
Emily: Thanks, that's very helpful.

 9
Emily: And what about the facilities in each room?
Receptionist: Well, we're a professional business and training centre and we have designed and equipped all our rooms to the highest standards. We can offer multimedia projectors, interactive whiteboards, wireless Internet, TV, video, DVD, laptops…All that you would expect from a professional training centre.
Emily: OK. Sounds good. And how are the rooms laid out?
Receptionist: We can be flexible. You can have whatever layout you like. Just let us know. I should also point out that all our main training rooms are of course air-conditioned.
Emily: And what arrangements are there for refreshments?
Receptionist: We can serve refreshments in the training rooms or in our special business centre restaurant. That seats 50 delegates, by the way.
Emily: And car parking?
Receptionist: We have free car parking for up to 70 cars. There's also disabled parking and I should also mention that we have all the other disabled facilities you would expect.
Emily: I am certainly very interested in making a booking. I'll check out your website and discuss everything with our managing director. There's one important thing we've not yet mentioned of course.
Receptionist: Yes I know, but I'm sure you'll find our prices very competitive! As a rough guide, we can offer…

 10
Receptionist: Century Business Centre. How can I help?
Emily: Good morning. It's Emily Maitland here again from ArrowInsurance. I'd like to discuss rates for using the centre on the date we spoke about.
Receptionist: Yes, certainly. I think I gave you an indication of our standard rates when we last spoke…
Emily: Yes, but I am working to quite a tight budget and unfortunately what you mentioned wouldn't be possible.
Receptionist: I think you'll find that our rates are very competitive.
Emily: Yes that may be the case, but I would need to have a lower price in order to be able to make a booking.
Receptionist: What sort of budget are you working to?
Emily: Let me just say that if you could reduce your standard rate by 15% it would be possible.
Receptionist: That's a rather big discount. One moment, let me have a word with the centre director…I've just had a word with the director and he says that we couldn't do such a large discount for a one-off booking, but if you could offer us some more business, he would make an exception to our normal policy.
Emily: Well, we are running other courses over the next couple of months and I would be pleased to hold them in the Century Business Centre if we could get a 15% discount on each booking.
Receptionist: I think we can do that. I'd need to check with my manager again but I think it would be OK if we can agree on dates.
Emily: OK. I'd like to take you up on that.

Unit 6

 11
Charles: OK, right…can we hear now what you've come up with? Can we start with you, Jerry?
Jerry: Yeah, sure. We thought it was important to have a checklist to help you plan. We felt that was crucial so you didn't forget to do something. So we would draw up a checklist of action points.
Charles: Thanks for that, Jerry. That's really interesting. A checklist – sure, that's important. Well, erm, who'd like to go next? Sally?
Sally: We spoke about lots of simple, practical points. For instance, we decided it was critical to be absolutely sure why you needed to have a meeting in the first place. We've been to lots of meetings which weren't really necessary – meetings that didn't have a clear focus. So we thought it was fundamental to decide first of all if a face-to-face meeting was needed. Could things be sorted out by email or by a video- or telephone conference?
Charles: Extremely interesting, Sally! Some very good points there. Thanks for that. OK, so who's going to go next? Sean?
Sean: OK, fine, well we thought it was essential to be clear what type of meeting it was. Obviously if it were formal, you would have to do things completely differently from if it were informal for just two or three people who were working together on the same project, for example.
Charles: Thanks Sean. That's a good comment. Can we bring you in now, Paul?
Paul: Well, we thought about having a checklist as well, but we also felt that it was vital to make sure that the venue for the meeting was appropriate. And linked to that, of course, is the question of equipment and facilities. It's no good not having a data projector if a presentation in the meeting requires one. And it's no good for a whole-day meeting if there aren't good facilities for serving food and drinks.
Charles: Thanks, Paul. Those are very good points. OK, well let's now compare what you've just brainstormed with the points I wanted to discuss…

 12
(see unit for the sentences)

Unit 7

 13
Vadim: Good morning. I'm Vadim Gyduk. I'm here for the AquaTec/Seamap meeting.
Receptionist: Good morning Mr Gyduk, let me just check your name off on the list. OK, that's fine. Here are the additional papers for the meeting and here is your name badge.
Vadim: Thanks very much. Where can I leave my overcoat?
Receptionist: You can leave your coat here in reception. No problem. I'm here all day.
Vadim: OK fine. And so where do I go now?
Receptionist: Coffee is being served in the Green Room on the third floor. The lift is over there.
Vadim: Thanks.

 14
1
Vadim: Hello, we haven't met before, have we? My name's Vadim Gyduk. I'm the production manager here in Bergen.
Sally: Hi, nice to meet you Vadim. Sally Wicks. I'm the president's PA.
Vadim: Pleased to meet you, Sally. How was your journey?
Sally: Uff…Not too good really. I flew in from New York to Stockholm late last night but I didn't get to Bergen till early this morning.
Vadim: Really! You must be pretty tired then.

2

Man: Hi Volker! Nice to see you again! How are you?
Volker: Very well, thank you. And you?
Man: Fine thanks. Better weather than when we met in New York. Winter in New York can really be something special!
Volker: But you know there's no such thing as bad weather. Only bad clothes!
Man: Yeah, right! How's your family by the way?
Volker: Well, my son's at university and my wife Mary has just started work. The house feels quite empty now.

3

George: Hi, I don't think we've met. I'm George Masterman. I'm one of Seamap's engineers.
Mark: Hi George, I'm Mark. Mark Field. I'm the marketing manager in New York.
George: Good to meet you, Mark. Are you staying near here?
Mark: Yes, I'm booked in at the Hilton. It's only five minutes' walk away.
George: So am I. I always like to book a hotel close to the conference centre. There's a shuttle bus every 15 minutes as well.
Mark: Oh, well, that's good.

4

Woman: Hi Debbie. Have you met Peter before?
Debbie: No, I don't think I have.
Woman: Aha…Well, Peter is in public relations.
Debbie: Nice to meet you, Peter.
Peter: I'm very pleased to meet you too, Debbie. You look fantastic! Nice skirt!

5

Man: Dan, let me introduce you to Sven. He's Seamap's commercial manager. Sven, this is Dan from the New York office.
Dan: We already know each other. Sven was at the first meeting we had six months ago. So what are you up to now then, Sven?
Sven: I've just got a new job – a promotion.
Dan: That's great news! Shall we have a chat over lunch?
Sven: Sure! Look forward to it.

15

Alina: Hello, have we met before?
Jane: No, I don't think so.
Alina: Well, my name's Alina Davey. I'm in the production team at AquaTec.
Jane: Hi, pleased to meet you, Alina. I'm Jane Searby.
Alina: Nice to meet you, Jane. Are you in production as well?
Jane: No, I'm in sales. I'm one of the sales reps. I work mainly in South America.
Alina: So you had quite a long journey to get here?
Jane: Yes, but I got a direct flight so it wasn't too bad.

16

Sven: Hi there. Long time no see!
Man: Hi Sven. Great to see you again!
Sven: So what are you up to now then?
Man: I've just got a new job. I'm the sales manager now.
Sven: Really! That's good news! Really good news. And how was your flight?
Man: Terrible. It was delayed for two hours.
Sven: Oh, sorry to hear that. Did you get a taxi from the airport?
Man: No. I got the hotel shuttle bus.
Sven: Are you staying near the conference centre then?
Man: Yeah, the hotel is right next door.
Sven: Can I get you another coffee, before we go into the meeting?
Man: No thanks. I'm fine.

Unit 8

17

Bernie: I think we're all here. That was pretty quick, thanks. I think we can launch proceedings now, so let's get the ball rolling. A warm welcome to everybody. On behalf of the whole AquaTec team, I'd like to say how pleased I am to meet up with our colleagues from Seamap. So a really warm welcome to the staff from Seamap! We've drawn up an agenda for the meeting. Does everybody have a copy? Is there anybody who didn't get a copy, by any chance? No? OK, great. Our administration seems to be working at last! OK, no more feeble jokes then, let's get this show on the road!

18

Bernie: Well, to start with, just a few formalities and some organizational matters. First of all Renate Bromma, our finance director, has sent her apologies. Unfortunately, she couldn't make the trip. She's snowed under with the quarterly sales figures. And Tony Adams, who works in design, had a sporting accident last week, so he's in hospital. OK then, so just looking round the table, I think I can see that everybody else is here. Yes…and so that just leaves me with the pleasant task of introducing my PA, Sally Wicks, to those who didn't have the pleasure of meeting her before the meeting. Sally is going to take the minutes. OK, so let's start by looking at the shape of the day. We're aiming to work through till one. And then we'll have a very short buffet lunch – just half an hour. And we plan to finish at three-ish, so that we can do a tour of the factory and warehouse before dinner. I hope, by the way, that everybody is able to join us for dinner.

19

(see unit for the words)

Unit 9

20

Stella: Would you like to start, Murat?
Murat: Yes, sure. I went to school in Georgia and after school I studied production engineering at a technical university in the capital, Tbilisi. My first job was as a railway engineer for the government. I worked on building the rail link between Tbilisi and the new international airport. Then two years ago, I moved to Dubai. I got a job as a design engineer for the new Dubai metro. Right now I'm working on the rail link between Dubai and the international airport. So it's a bit like the job I did at home in Georgia, but I'm paid ten times more!

21

Stella: Great! Thanks very much, Murat. Would you like to continue, Cam?
Cam: Absolutely. I was born in Vietnam and went to school and college there. Later, I left Vietnam to go to Hong Kong because I'm actually Chinese. I worked in Hong Kong for a year as a salesperson in a store and then I went to England. In England I got a job as a trainee store manager. I did that for a couple of years and then joined an airline as one of the trainee cabin staff. I mainly flew on the long haul flights to China. Last year the company offered me a job as office manager with the ground staff in Dubai. So that's why I'm here today.

22

Stella: Thanks Cam. A very varied career to say the least! Over to you now, Andre. I'm conscious of the time, so could you focus on just the main facts, please? We need to make sure we have enough time for everybody.
Andre: OK, I'll be as brief as possible. My story is a bit unusual as well. I was born in the Congo, but when I was 18 my uncle sent me to St Petersburg in Russia to study medicine. I finally got a degree in tropical medicine. After my studies I got married and went with my Russian wife to Berlin in Germany. I wanted to work as a doctor there, but they wouldn't accept my Russian qualifications and so I got a job working for a German pharmaceutical company as a sales rep. Because of my languages – I speak English, French, German and Russian – the company offered me the opportunity of a job in the UAE. I've been working here for three years now – I promote the company's products mainly in the English and German hospitals and medical centres. So I have to travel quite a lot for my work.

23

(see unit for the words)

Listening scripts 101

Unit 10

24

Stella: I'd like to say just a few words about today's agenda. This year we decided to hold a meeting for all new mystery hotel guests rather than briefing people over the phone as we've done previously. The aim of this meeting is to prepare you to do the audits effectively and also we thought it would be good for you to meet each other, so that you realize that you are part of a team and not just working in isolation. So can I ask you all to look at the agenda please. OK. So we've all introduced ourselves. That was item 1. So now let's look at item 2. Under item 2 I'd like to talk about the hotel chains we're going to audit. You'll be pleased to hear that we now have contracts with five of the major hotel companies here. Then under item 3 we need to focus on how the audits are conducted and look at the audit documents. Item 3 will be the longest part of our meeting. Fourthly, I will clarify salary and expenses for you. The fifth item on the agenda is to decide who does what and when, the allocation of hotels to mystery guests and the schedules for visits. Then, under any other business, I'd like to mention a new development we're planning for the summer. More about that later! Does anyone have anything else you'd like to discuss under AOB? No? OK, just feel free to add something at any time during the meeting, if you think of anything. OK, any questions about the agenda or anything else, before we make a start?

25

Stella: OK then. Let me talk you through item 2 – the hotel chains we're contracted to audit. I have prepared a summary document, which gives you all the details of the hotel chains and the names and locations of the individual hotels. As you can see, it's a pretty impressive portfolio of clients...

[pause]

Stella: Does anyone have any further questions at this point about the hotel chains? Or can we move on? OK, if that covers item 2, let's turn to the next item. As I said before, item 3 will probably be the most time-consuming. I've asked the person who has been working on the new audit documents to talk us through them. Ian Benson is CF Audits' marketing manager and he is a real expert on the documentation and how to use it. He should be here any minute now. He's probably stuck in the Dubai traffic! While we're waiting, I'll just say a few words about – Ah! Hello Ian!
Ian: Hi Stella. Sorry for being late. The traffic was terrible!

Stella: Good to see you! I've just introduced you to the group, so if you don't mind, I think we can go straight into your contribution. Would you like to talk us through the audit documents? And then take us through the method of working?
Ian: Yes, sure. No problem. Good morning everybody. First of all, I'd like to reassure you that we have cut back the documentation considerably this year. The changes resulted from very good feedback from our auditors, based on their first-hand practical experience doing the job. So the whole package has been streamlined based on their comments and should be very easy to use. If you could all open the booklet on page three, I'll...

[pause]

Stella: Well thank you very much, Ian, for such a clear presentation of the audit process. I think that really ties up that topic very neatly. That definitely thoroughly covers that item. Thank you very much for taking the time to come and talk to us. I think all that remains now is to let you rejoin another Dubai traffic jam!
Ian: Thanks, OK, bye everybody. I look forward to reading your audit reports!
Delegates: Bye.
Stella: Goodbye Ian and thanks again. Well I think that's all we need to say about that issue at the moment. Obviously feel free to contact me at any time if you have questions, when you are doing the audits. OK, so that brings us to the next item. Item 4. Let's take up the important topic of salary and expenses. Again you have a summary of the main points on the paper I've just passed round. As you can see, all travel costs to and from the hotels are met in full. We also reimburse you for all reasonable expenses in the hotels. Accommodation, drinks, meals, and so on…So basically you don't spend any of your own money from the point you leave home until you return. Now the fee for each audit depends on the size of the hotel and the number of nights you stay there. Obviously you can do most audits in 24 hours …

[pause]

Stella: OK. I think that covers expenses and fees. So following that, shall we turn to the allocation of hotels now? Let's move on to item 5. This should be fairly short. Let me first of all explain the principle we use to make the allocations. We try as far as possible to give you the hotels that fit into your existing work schedule. So if you know that you will have to travel to Abu Dhabi in April, we allocate you a hotel there for a convenient date. Is that clear?

[pause]

Stella: Well, I think the allocation issue seems to be resolved. Obviously I can't give you your final allocations today. That will take time to organize, but I think we've cleared up all the key points at this stage. So, any more questions at this point? No? OK I think we can move on again. That brings us finally to AOB – any other business. As I said at the beginning of the meeting, I'd like to mention here a new and very exciting development we're planning for the summer. You'll be very pleased to hear that we…

26

(see unit for the sentences)

Unit 11

27

Natasha: Good morning everybody. It's Natasha here. Can I first check a few technical details? Can you all hear me? Is anybody having problems with the sound or picture quality? What about you in Italy, Nando?
Nando: Good morning Natasha. No problem with the sound here in Milan. The picture quality is fine as well.
Natasha: Thanks Nando. And what about Stefan in Berlin?
Stefan: Hi Natasha. The sound here is a bit faint but I can see you clearly. No problem with the picture.
Natasha: Thanks Stefan. Now over to London. How are things with you, Roger?
Roger: Good morning Natasha. The picture is a bit dark, but no problem really. And the sound is crystal clear.
Natasha: Great, Roger. Thanks. And finally over to Madrid. Good morning Carmen. Everything OK?
Carmen: Good morning Natasha. The picture here is very dark and a bit distorted as well. And the sound is delayed and a bit crackly, so I miss every other word. I don't think the quality is good enough for the conference.
Natasha: Thanks for that, Carmen. I'll redial and we'll see if we can sort out the problems.
Carmen: Thanks.
Natasha: Is that any better now, Carmen?
Carmen: Yes, it's fine now.
Natasha: OK, great. Let's make a start, shall we?

28

Natasha: Welcome to the meeting, everybody. Right, now before we start, I'd like to make a few general points by way of introduction. I realize that there is some dissatisfaction about the new logo and the proposed marketing campaign. That is one of the reasons we have organized this morning's conference call. This is your opportunity to tell us how you feel about the proposals and to give us your general input and suggestions for improving things. I don't want to be too heavy-handed, but I realize that some of our discussion might be a bit heated so I would like to set some ground rules to help us move forward constructively. Firstly a very, very basic point – could I ask you all not to interrupt when someone else is talking? We all know that interruptions are not helpful in face-to-face meetings and they are doubly difficult to cope with in a videoconference. Equally, if you want to speak, can you raise a hand, so that I can call you in at an appropriate time? So then, the rule is that we speak one at a time, so you all have the chance to put your views forward. OK? And secondly, if we disagree about something, could we try and make our disagreement positive? So instead of just saying that something is rubbish, can we suggest an alternative? OK, that's enough of me being a school teacher. So let's make a start. I suggest that each person gives his or her opinion first and then we have a discussion round the table.

29
(see unit for the sentences)

Unit 12

30
Natasha: OK, Nando. Can I ask you to start off? Maybe, if you limit your comments to the new logo to start with?
Nando: Sure, that's fine. Well, I understand that since the company took over 'Well Body' our range of products has increased but, well, personally, I don't think that the company should change its logo. As I see it, our core business is the same. I don't know how the others feel but I think we should keep the old Tara logo. It is so well-known and respected in the market. And I also think that the online marketing strategy is completely wrong.
Natasha: Let's not go into that now, Nando. We'll come to that later on. I don't want to get sidetracked at this stage. What are your views about the logo, Stefan?
Stefan: I totally agree with Nando. I'm completely against changing the logo. Don't get me wrong, I can see what the company is trying to do, but the trouble is, if we change the logo, I think we risk losing some of our market share. And I agree with Nando about online marketing…
Natasha: Can we discuss that later please? I don't want to get off the point. Let's stick to the logo at the moment, if we can. Would you like to come in now, Roger?
Roger: You know, I tend to agree with my colleagues about the logo. In my opinion there's no need to fix something that's not broken…I suggest keeping the Tara logo… If you ask me, I think we should keep our old logo.
Carmen: Can I come in now please?
Natasha: Yes sure, Carmen. I think the others have made their views on the logo pretty clear.
Carmen: Yes, well I think we have to move with the times. I don't think we can ignore the fact that we are now selling a lot of new Well Body products. Can I make a suggestion? I'm against changing the logo completely, for all the reasons given by the others. How about keeping the basic design of the Tara logo, but giving it a new, modern, fresh look by just changing the colours? I recommend we adapt the logo to the colour scheme of the new packaging. What do you think?
Natasha: That's a very interesting suggestion, Carmen. Well, thanks to everybody for being so frank – that's given me lots to think about regarding the logo. I'll take your views and Carmen's suggestion back to the board. OK, now shall we move on at last to the topic of online marketing? I know that many of you…

31
Let's not go into that now.
We'll come on to that later.
I don't want to get sidetracked at this stage.
Can we discuss that later please?
I don't want to get off the point.
Let's stick to the logo at the moment if we can.
Can I make a suggestion?
I recommend we adapt the logo.
How about keeping the basic design?
I suggest keeping the Tara logo.
Shall we move on?
I think we should keep our old logo.

Unit 13

32
Boris: We all know why we are having this meeting today. So straight to the point! The economic situation is terrible. A disaster. You've all seen the quarterly sales figures. We're 30% down on the same time last year. The forecast for the next quarter looks even worse. We are in real financial difficulty. We must come up with a strategy to stop the rot. We must make savings or we'll be bankrupt by the end of the year. And we must start today. There's no time to waste!

33
Boris: Sorry again about that misunderstanding. Thanks for agreeing to go through our proposals. Our main proposal is to cut staff at all levels. The advantages would be that we could make big savings and they would be immediate.
Karl: Sorry for cutting in again Boris, but there are lots of disadvantages too. What do you think, Jason?
Jason: There sure are. The main problem would be possible strikes. There could be staff unrest. Maybe even sabotage at the mills.
Karl: Yeah, I agree with Jason. Wouldn't it be better if–
Boris: Yes, but if we want to make big cuts the only way to do it is redundancies on a large scale. None of the problems mentioned by Jason worry me or my colleagues. What do you say, Andrej?
Andrej: We can control any staff problems. We've got very good security. We've got very well-trained security staff. With the best equipment.
Boris: Do you agree, Michail?
Michail: Absolutely. We've got enough security to protect the mills and deal with problems.
Boris: OK then. Can I continue with our ideas?
Karl: Sure, we're listening.
Boris: Well, we propose to fire 50% of the mill workers next Friday – without warning. They'll get their pay and be told to leave and not return to work again. There'll be no redundancy pay but we'll offer a bonus of one week's pay at the end of the month to everybody who goes quietly and without trouble.
Karl: You'll never get away with that!
Boris: Just wait and see. Our security department has already been given a list of those who'll go and we have plans for the security staff to be in position to deal with any troublemakers. They'll take up positions in the mills all weekend and for longer if necessary.

34
Boris: Now we also have plans for cutting the American staff.
Karl: I was expecting that! Well, go ahead!
Boris: Well, as you know, we have 55 American engineers and managers. Most of them are on three- to four-year contracts and very high salaries. They have generally done a very good job in training the Russian managers in new approaches and modern technology. But as a group they cost a lot. We are paying for luxury apartments for them in the centre of the city. They each have a personal driver and an interpreter. They're just too expensive for the company in the present financial crisis.
Karl: I hope you're not planning to deal with them in the same way as with the Russian workers.
Boris: No, of course not. Our suggestion is that we tell you how many we want to lose and you tell us how best to do it.
Karl: Very clever, Boris. Go on, what's the bottom line?
Boris: OK. We must lose between 30 and 40 by the end of the year. We feel they have done their job well over the three years and most of the Russian managers can now do the work on their own without support.

35
(see unit for the sentences)

Unit 14

36

Karl: Well guys, I know this must all be a terrible shock to you. I just hope that we can find a solution that can accommodate as many people as possible. Shall we try and focus on the positive points? Firstly, all of you only have seven months of your contracts to run. And again, looking at this positively, you've already achieved your main objective of training up the Russian employees. Can I get some reaction from you now? Would you like to start, Andrew?
Andrew: Well, I'm not all that surprised to hear about the poor financial situation. I've been aware for some time that the demand for paper pulp has got less. What really shocks me though, is the way the company wants to deal with the problem. The cutbacks are really severe.
Karl: Thanks for that, Andrew. Could I ask you to come in now, Tony? What do you think?
Tony: To be blunt, I think the way the company is acting is criminal! It shouldn't be possible to do this sort of thing nowadays.
Karl: What's the main problem for you, Tony? What's the main thing you don't like about this?
Tony: Maybe the worst thing for me is the way the company is treating the Russian employees. It's just not right. It's not modern, civilized practice.
Karl: OK. Right. And you, Sam. What are your thoughts?
Sam: I just agree with Tony and Andrew. I think the whole business stinks.
Karl: OK. OK. I get the message. Look, I know you all feel strongly about this, but as I say, I think you can look at it in two ways: yes, your contracts are being ended ahead of time, but on the other hand, I think that reflects how quickly you've achieved your objectives here.

37
(see unit for the sentences)

Unit 15

38

Bill: Morning everybody. Well, as you know, we've just won the contract to redesign Sanita's new website. You all know what the old website is like and we need to come up with a new concept. I don't want to say too much more at this stage. I'd prefer to go straight into brainstorming mode. I don't want to be criticized again for wanting to do things the way we did them in the seventies, when I started in this business! So over to you!…What, has nobody got anything to say? Come on, let's hear a few of your ideas. You normally have so much to say…OK, well if nobody is going to volunteer a comment, I'm going to have to pick on individuals…OK, over to my first victim then! Sheila, let's hear some of your ideas about this.
Sheila: Sorry for making life hard for you, Bill. It's quite early and I didn't get my cup of coffee this morning – I guess my brain isn't quite in brainstorming mode yet. Anyway, erm…for me, I think the old website doesn't focus enough on the range of services the company offers. From hospitals to care homes to health and travel insurance.
Bill: Thanks for that, Sheila. Feel free to help yourself to a coffee from the machine. OK, so to clarify, we need to highlight the wide range of services.
Sheila: Yes, that's right.
Bill: OK, so I'll carry on picking on people if that's OK. Tom?
Tom: I'd like to suggest that we make a big point about the 24-hour telephone advice service. It's important for people to know they can get help whenever they need it.
Bill: Good idea, Tom. Thanks. So over to you now, Brenda.
Brenda: Well, linked to Tom's suggestion, there's the free, online health information service from Sanita's medical experts. And let's not forget the health check service. That's a big selling point.
Bill: Great. So here's what we've come up with so far. Firstly the range of services, secondly the 24-hour telephone service, the free online information service and the health check service. OK?
Tom: Yes. And most important for me, the special services for children, like children's nurseries and children's hospitals.
Brenda: Also the dental service. It's crucial to stress that as well.
Sheila: I think we've overlooked the price of membership. That could also be a big selling point.
Bill: It could indeed, Sheila. In my time we wouldn't have focused on something as basic as price, but in the modern age it's obviously very relevant. It's the main thing that most people think about nowadays. OK, so I'll just run through what we've suggested so far. I think we've come up with several major areas. Firstly, the wide range of services, secondly…

39
(see answer key for the sentences)

40
(see unit for the sentences)

Unit 16

41

Bill: Good morning everybody. It's good to be back with you again. We've got quite a lot to talk through today and we also want to show you a sample home page. Let me make it clear at this stage that all the material is in draft form and we welcome your feedback so that we can be sure to produce a really high quality product that fully meets all your needs. Please feel free to stop me and ask questions at any time during my presentation. Any questions so far? No? Right then…

42

Bill: So as you can imagine, we are suggesting some big changes!
Sandra: That's a pretty damning criticism of our current home page, Bill! Can I just ask you to run through that again please? Could you tell us a little bit more about priorities especially? I think that would help us to understand your new concept a bit better.
Bill: Sure, no problem. What I'm trying to say is that we think that most people who come to the website for the first time are only interested in one thing. They want to know how much it costs, so that needs to jump off the page. Let me put it another way: all the information on the home page about products and services is just too confusing. In other words, just keep that first message simple. Does that clarify things?
Sandra: Thanks for that, Bill. That's very clear.
Bill: OK, great. So to carry on, the first thing we've put on the home page is a positive picture of a happy smiling family. We need to communicate the healthy lifestyle visually. No words. Then we hit them with your great offers! Free 3-month trial offer! 50% no claims bonus! Insure one child and all other children are free. Again the magic word 'free'! Then we have two links to other pages. The first is 'ten reasons for joining Sanita' and the second is a 'frequently asked questions' button.
Sandra: So what you're saying is that we have nothing about our products and services on the home page? Is that right?
Bill: Yeah, that's it. We keep the home page simple with a focus only on price and free offers. Have I made that clear enough?
Sandra: Is that clear to everybody?
Delegates: Yes.
Bill: Excellent. Let's have a look at the prototype home page then. As you can see…

43
(see unit for the sentences)

Unit 17

44

Chairman: Well Veronica, I'd like to try to summarize what we've been discussing so far this morning. I think it's best if I just run through the main points we've agreed. OK?

Veronica: Yes, that makes sense. I think it's pretty clear what we've decided but it's always better to summarize decisions formally. Just in case. Just to be absolutely sure about the next steps.
Chairman: Right, I think we have come up with two, possibly three, projects for the first six months of the year. Firstly, we've agreed that we'll make a 30-minute documentary about very unusual English weddings. Is that right?
Veronica: Yes, that's correct. My first job then is to research some unusual situations and get back to you by the end of January with the ideas for your approval. Ideally you like the idea of weddings in unusual locations – on mountain tops, in trees, under water, and so on.
Chairman: Yes that's right, but we also like the idea of a wedding in a medieval castle with knights in armour on horses and that sort of thing…If we could manage it, that would look really spectacular! Does anyone have anything else to add on this?
Japanese director: Yes, I agree with that. Our viewers really like English history. They like the costumes and the traditions.
Chairman: Can I ask you then, Veronica, to look into the possibility of filming a medieval wedding?
Veronica: Sure, no problem. As I said, I'll do my best to have some firm suggestions by the end of January.
Chairman: Thanks very much. OK, so moving on, the next project is a short film on the life of Rudyard Kipling. We said we wanted this to be filmed partly in the Kipling family home in the south of England.
Veronica: Yes, so my task when I return is to check that we can get permission to film there. The house is a museum now. I don't think there will be a problem but it might be expensive.
Chairman: So you'll check that by what date, Veronica?
Veronica: I'll ring as soon as I get back and I should be able to give you an answer by the end of next week. Is that OK?
Chairman: That's fine. OK, that brings us to the last point. We said that we would also possibly like to do a documentary about an open-air museum. The ideal location would be the Black Country Museum near Birmingham.
Veronica: That's right. Again, I need to check with the museum to see if they will agree to it. It's complicated because the museum is like a small town with shops, a church, a school, factories, a pub, a fish and chip shop, and so on. If we want to film there, we'll need to get permission from all the people who work there. It won't be easy. Anyway, I'll try my best.

45
Chairman: OK, that brings us to the end of all the items on the agenda. Are there any further points you would like to discuss? Is there any other business for the meeting?
Veronica: Yes, under any other business I'd like to talk about accommodation and travel expenses for the camera crews. Is that possible?
Chairman: Yes, it's possible, but I think that's something we can sort out by email. Could you send me a few details and I'll get back to you as soon as I can.
Veronica: Yes sure, no problem. I've already written a report about it. I can send you a copy at the end of the meeting.
Chairman: Fine. OK then. If there's nothing else to discuss I'd like to fix a date for our next meeting with Veronica. I think the best thing would be to organize a videoconference at the end of January to see where we are with the projects. Veronica, can you manage the 30th of January?
Veronica: Yes, that's fine for me.
Chairman: Is that date OK for everybody else? Yes? OK, I would suggest that we start the conference at 6am GMT. A good early start for you, Veronica!
Veronica: Don't worry about me. I understand the difficulties with the time difference only too well!
Chairman: And I assume that time is convenient for everybody else? OK? I think we've covered everything, so if nobody has anything to add I think we can stop there. It just remains for me to thank Veronica for her excellent contribution, as usual. I look forward to seeing you again at the next videoconference. Have a safe journey home.

46
(see unit for the sentences)

Unit 18

47
President: Good morning everybody. I'm delighted to see so many of you present. As I mentioned in my email, it's crucial that we have a quorum today because we have to make some very important decisions affecting the expansion of the company in South America and Asia over the next two years. Firstly though, a few administrative matters. We have apologies from Tony Jefferson and Isabel Marron. They are both unwell but have authorized two other colleagues to make their proxy votes on the franchise applications. OK then. Can I sign the minutes of the last meeting as a correct record?
Solange: I'm not sure, but I think there may be a small error on page 1. Item 2. I think we agreed to take action in December, not in March next year.
President: Thanks for that, Solange. Yes, I think you're right. That's how I remember it as well. Does everybody else agree? Yes? OK. Can you make the change, Rachel? OK then. May I sign the minutes now? OK? Thanks. And are there any items arising from the minutes?
Ruprecht: I can report that all action points have been carried out by the required deadline.
President: Thanks very much, Ruprecht. That's very helpful. OK, I think we can start…

48
President: OK. So you had copies of summaries of the three reports before the meeting and you've just had the opportunity to hear the full reports. So you've had all the necessary background information on which to base your decisions about the franchise applications. Now it's time to hear your views on their strengths and weaknesses. So over to you! OK, so who would like to start? Lisa Marra? Could we hear the Italian perspective from you?
Lisa: Yes, sure. For me it's pretty clear-cut. The visit to the South American clubs made it quite clear that their current premises are not up to Move It standards. Also, the equipment in a lot of the clubs is very old and not always 100% safe. The financial situation of the group of potential investors in Chile is also not secure enough. They don't have the necessary capital to develop the clubs along Move It lines. The investors in Asia seem in a much stronger position and they have already done a lot of market research, so I feel quite confident about them joining the Move It family.
President: You've expressed your point of view very clearly as usual, Lisa. Many thanks for starting off the discussion so decisively. Who else would like to come in at this point? Thomas Pinkhaus, maybe you'd like to come in now?
Thomas: About time, I thought you were never going to get round to me! Well, our Lisa here is a smart cookie and she has made a few good points. Yeah, I think the health and safety issues about the premises in Chile and Argentina are a whopping great problem. But you know, the situation in Asia as Lisa has just said is much better. It would sure be good to hear what my fellow directors think.
President: There is a place for a more relaxed and informal approach, Thomas, but I suggest not in our board meetings.
Thomas: Sorry. It won't happen again.
President: OK. Let's move on then. Well, I can see from Ruprecht's facial expression that he is keen to come in here. Ruprecht, would you like to say a few words about this?
Ruprecht: Well, I was interested to hear what Lisa and Thomas said but I really

think they are overstating the importance of the present condition of the club premises in Chile and Argentina. With the support of the Move It organization they could greatly improve the situation over the next year, I think. And it would be relatively simple to make the buildings safe in case of fire. So in my opinion…

 49

(see unit for the text)

50

President: Well, that brings us to the vote. Do we accept or reject the various applications? I propose we vote on each set of applications separately. Is that accepted? Yes, Ruprecht – do you wish to come in here?
Ruprecht: On a point of order, I'd like to say that I am in favour of considering each application separately, but I would like to propose a specific order. I would like to vote on the less controversial applications first. So I would suggest we start with the applications from Asia and then go on to those from South America.
President: I am happy to accept that proposal unless there are any objections. OK. Can I take it that Ruprecht's proposal is accepted? No, you'd like to say something Lisa?
Lisa: Yes, I would suggest that we vote on the franchise applications from Hong Kong, Beijing, Tokyo and Osaka in one block and that we then vote on the applications from the clubs in Chile and Argentina separately.
President: OK, so we now have a very concrete proposal from Lisa. Could I have a seconder? Solange?
Solange: Yes, I'm happy to second the proposal.
President: OK, so the motion is that we accept the franchise applications from Hong Kong, Beijing, Tokyo and Osaka. I now formally put the motion to the vote. Raise your hands if you are in favour… Raise your hands if you are against…Any abstentions? No? I hereby declare that the motion was carried and the vote was unanimous when we include the two proxy votes. And now onto the clubs in Chile and Argentina.
Lisa: I would like to put forward the proposal that we reject their applications.
Ruprecht: I'd like to propose a major amendment to the motion before we vote. I'd like to propose the motion that we accept the applications from the clubs in Chile and Argentina, but for a two-year period only. I further propose that the applications should be reviewed again at the end of two years and that they should only be extended if the clubs meet Move It standards relating to health and safety, and quality of premises.
President: Do I have a seconder for Ruprecht's motion? Thomas?
Thomas: Yes, I second the motion.
President: OK, I put the motion formally to the group. All those in favour? All those against? Does anybody wish to abstain? Well that's very close. In fact, it's a 50-50 split. So I am going to use the chairman's casting vote in favour of the motion. So, I hereby declare that the motion was carried.

 51

(see unit for the sentences)

Unit 19

52

Kim: I think it's important to write minutes very carefully because they need to be an accurate record of what took place and what decisions were taken. They are also useful because people can easily forget what was decided at a meeting if nothing is written down.
Serge: In my opinion, it's essential to write the minutes immediately after the meeting and the next day at the latest. They should then be circulated straight away in order to remind those who attended about action points.
Laura: I think one of the most important things when writing minutes is to avoid writing anything which could embarrass anyone. It's important always to be positive. I never write, for example, that the discussion was angry or aggressive. I prefer to say that it was lively or energetic.

53

agreed	explained
asked	promised
brought up	raised
complained	recommended
decided	reported
discussed	stressed
emphasized	suggested

Unit 20

54

Jack: It's essential that an action plan should contain three elements. These are the action points which need to be achieved, the person or persons who should complete the tasks, and the date for completion. The deadline for action point 1, finishing the marketing report, is the 17th of May. Action point 2 needs to be finished by the 30th of May. The new marketing material needs to be ready by the 30th of June. The deadline for completing the new website is the 15th of June. Finally, the training course for marketing and sales staff needs to be ready by the 30th of June.

55

Jo: Jo Calderwood.
Alan: Hi Jo, this is Alan from head office. I was just wondering how things were progressing with the action points. Can we go through them one by one?
Jo: Sure, no problem. Fire away.
Alan: Well, how is the report progressing?
Jo: That's going really well. I'll be finished by the end of the week. Two weeks ahead of schedule.
Alan: Great! Good to hear that. And the sales strategy?
Jo: Well that's taking a bit longer than we thought, but it will be ready by the deadline on the 30th of May.
Alan: That's good news as well. So on to the marketing material. Is that finished yet?
Jo: No not yet, but we are just about to do a photo shoot, next Monday. Don't worry though, it will be completed before the end of June.
Alan: Another piece of good news! Have you got any bad news?
Jo: Well no, not exactly bad, but the website is a bit behind schedule. I don't think we'll make the deadline. I think we'll be about a week late in finishing that.
Alan: OK, but is the preparation for the training course progressing well?
Jo: No problem there. The outline is already complete.
Alan: OK, thanks for all your good work…

56

Jack: There are usually action points after most meetings. Sometimes the action points are written in the minutes and at other times they are separate documents attached to the minutes. One of the first things the chairperson should do at the next meeting is to check whether the actions have been completed by persons as agreed. This check, however, is not the only way of monitoring action. In fact, if this is the only check, it could lead to problems. Usually most chairpersons arrange for there to be an ongoing check and monitoring of progress towards achieving the agreed action points. Sometimes monitoring to see if people are sticking to the agreed deadlines takes place in follow-up meetings. Sometimes the chairperson or another manager may ask people to write a progress report, and in extreme cases a manager may ring up every day to check on progress! Often this monitoring can also help the people who are completing the tasks, because it gives them the opportunity to ask questions for clarification or information, or even to negotiate an extension to the deadline.

Answer key

Unit 1

1.
1 Rick Casbon → Uwe Timm
2 Tom Buddell → Paul Hoffman
3 Jenny Tidman → Paul Hoffman
4 Uwe Timm → Jenny Tidman
5 Uwe Timm → Rick Casbon
6 Uwe Timm → Jenny Tidman
7 Jenny Tidman → Paul Hoffman

2.
a 2   e 7
b 4   f 3
c 1   g 5
d 6

3.
1 F 2 T 3 T 4 F 5 T 6 F

5.
annual general meeting (AGM): 2
progress meeting: 7
board meeting: 1
team meeting: 6
brainstorming meeting: 5
staff appraisal meeting: 4
training meeting: 3

6.
1 g   3 b   5 c   7 a
2 e   4 f   6 d

8.
1 up   3 on   5 for   7 of
2 through 4 at   6 about   8 with

Unit 2

1.
1 a   3 e   5 f   7 b
2 c   4 g   6 d

3.

Who?	What?	When?
1 Jenny Tidman/ Paul Hoffman	Staff development meeting	15th July
2 Uwe Timm/ Rick Casbon	AGM	12th November
3 Uwe Timm/ Paul Hoffman	Team meeting	Thursday, 9.30–10.30am
4 Uwe Timm/ Jenny Tidman	Brainstorming meeting	Wednesday, 4pm
5 Rick Casbon/ Uwe Timm	Videoconference	Friday, 3pm GMT
6 Uwe Timm/ Jenny Tidman	Appraisal meeting	Thursday 2nd April, 7am

4.
1 f   3 d   5 g   7 e
2 c   4 a   6 h   8 b

5.
1 Yes, I can make that date.
2 Yes, I'm free on that date.
3 Tuesday at nine o'clock is fine for me.
4 Sorry, I can't make the meeting next week.
5 I'm afraid not, I'm away on a business trip.
6 Wednesday the 15th at 11 o'clock sounds good.
7 Yes sure, how about Monday 8th or Tuesday 9th?
8 Yes, I'm happy with next Monday morning.
9 I'm afraid I have another appointment then.
10 Yes, that date works for me.

7.
1 Can   4 do, think
2 need, is   5 have
3 am

8.
Conversation 1: d, a, f, c, e, b
Conversation 2: e, d, b, c, f, a

9.
1 next week   7 board members
2 business trip   8 in mind
3 get back   9 of the 15th
4 Tuesday 9th   10 I'll try
5 o'clock   11 16.00 GMT
6 for me   12 problem

Unit 3

1.
1 C   3 D   5 A   7 A
2 A   4 B,C 6 C,D

2.
Email A is the most formal.
Email C is the most informal.

3.
Formal: Dear colleagues, / I trust you are all well. / Please find herewith / I detail below / I would advise / With best regards. (*can also be informal depending on the context*) / Yours sincerely, / I look forward to seeing you / for your perusal / Please find attached
Informal: Dear Jenny, (*can also be more formal depending on the context*) / It was good to speak the other day. / Best wishes, (*can also be more formal depending on the context*) / Hello Jenny, / I finally got round to writing to you. / Sorry for the long delay. / I have really been snowed under / better late than never / down to business / plus / I've attached / See you on Thursday. / Cheers for now, / Hi Uwe, / I'm looking forward to our meeting / All the best,

4.
1 Salina   3 Salina   5 Tony
2 Jeremy   4 Olga   6 Marmen

8.
1 I am looking forward to meeting you next week.
2 Our biggest client is visiting today.
3 Is the printer working?
4 He is not sitting in his office.
5 Are you coming to the meeting?

Unit 4

1.
1 go over   7 confirm
2 right   8 after
3 note   9 check
4 forget   10 back
5 see   11 forward
6 decided

3.
1 Can I check the details of the meeting with you again?
2 Let me make a note of the date and the time before I forget.
3 So I'll see you on Wednesday at four o'clock in your office, OK?
4 Let me just go over that again.
5 I'm looking forward to seeing you on the 5th at 10 o'clock.

4.
Correct order: b, e, c, f, a, h, g, i, d

5.
1 Because he has got a job with another company.
2 An IT consultant.

6.
1 cancel
2 postpone

8.
1 a   2 e   3 d   4 c   5 b

Unit 5

1.
1 management training course
2 June 13th
3 about 30
4 Room 1 = 48; Room 2 = 36; Room 3 = 16; Room 4 = 8

2.
1 booking   4 looking   7 split
2 availability 5 need   8 provisional
3 mind   6 delegates   9 available

3.
Facilities mentioned: multimedia projector, interactive whiteboard, wireless Internet, television, video, DVD, laptop, restaurant, car park

4.

1	through	5	equipped
2	holds	6	professional
3	floor	7	serve
4	facilities	8	seats

6.
Yes, she accepts the final offer.

7.

1	rates	7	15%
2	indication	8	discount
3	budget	9	one-off
4	competitive	10	exception
5	booking	11	manager
6	working	12	up

9.

1	need	4	Could
2	must	5	should
3	can		

10.

1 c   2 e   3 a   4 b   5 d

Unit 6

1.

1	on	3	of	5	to
2	of	4	as	6	to

3.
Points mentioned: 1, 2, 7, 8, 10

4.

1	Paul	4	Paul
2	Sean	5	Sally
3	Jerry		

5.

1	crucial	4	essential
2	critical	5	vital
3	fundamental		

8.

1	f	3	e	5	d
2	c	4	a	6	b

10.

1	Weak	3	Strong	5	Weak
2	Strong	4	Weak	6	Strong

11.

1	came up with	3	stick to
2	drawn up	4	sorted out

Unit 7

1.
Sentences mentioned: 1, 2, 5, 6, 9, 10, 11, 13, 14

3.

1 physical appearance
2 family
3 salary
4 refreshments
5 travel to the meeting
6 sport

4.
Not appropriate for small talk: feelings, physical appearance, salary, religion, politics. Family and jobs should also be avoided unless talking more generally or with someone that you know a little better.

6.

1 travel to the meeting
2 weather (and family)
3 accommodation
4 physical appearance
5 jobs

Conversation 4 is not appropriate because Peter refers to Debbie's physical appearance (her skirt).

7.

1	e	3	b	5	h	7	c
2	d	4	a	6	g	8	f

8.
Correct order: c, g, d, a, h, f, b, e

11.

1 Let's meet for a drink.
2 Shall we chat over lunch?
3 Let's go and have a coffee.
4 Shall we sit over there?
5 Let's get a taxi back to the hotel.

Unit 8

1.

1	colleagues	4	attention
2	Sorry	5	discuss
3	fun	6	time

The chairman uses the friendly, less formal phrase 'Sorry to interrupt your fun' to get people's attention.

2.

1	making your way	4	agenda
2	fun	5	to introduce
3	colleagues	6	to interrupt

3.
He mentions the agenda. It is an important document because it is the plan of the meeting.

4.
I think we can launch proceedings now. F
Let's get the ball rolling. I
Let's get this show on the road! I

He uses some informal language to make people feel comfortable and relaxed.

5.

1	Agenda	4	Date and time
2	Objective	5	Participants
3	Venue	6	Apologies

6.

1 She is snowed under with the quarterly sales figures.
2 She is going to take the minutes.
3 They are having a very short buffet lunch – just half an hour.
4 They are doing a tour of the factory and warehouse.

7.
Things that Bernie does: 1, 3, 5, 6, 7, 8, 10

8.

1 take the minutes
2 snowed under
3 has sent her apologies
4 we're aiming
5 the shape of the day
6 looking round the table
7 a few formalities

9.
Correct order: n, l, j, f, q, b, g, h, p, k, o, d, m, a, i, e, c

10.

designer   director
president   PA
administrator

11.

1 My PA has drawn up the agenda.
2 The finance director has sent his/her apologies.
3 Sally has not distributed the minutes.
4 We have opened a new factory.
5 He has had a sporting accident.

Unit 9

1.

1	was	5	worked
2	moved	6	joined
3	completed	7	started
4	went		

3.

1	F	3	F	5	T	7	T
2	F	4	F	6	T		

4.

1 a   2 a   3 a   4 b

5.

1 The Congo
2 St Petersburg, Russia
3 English, French, German and Russian
4 Sales rep (for a German pharmaceutical company)

6.

1 My first job was as an engineer.
2 I was born in New York and went to school in Washington.
3 Two years ago I got a job as manager of a hotel in Hong Kong.
4 After school I studied medicine at university in Liverpool.
5 I started my current job last year.
6 Now I'm a doctor in a hospital in France.

8.
/d/: joined, offered, travelled, moved
/ɪd/: started, studied, wanted, accepted
/t/: worked, introduced

9.

Regular verbs		Irregular verbs	
Infinitive	Past simple 'I'	Infinitive	Past simple 'I'
to study	I studied	to go	I went
to work	I worked	to be	I was
to move	I moved	to get	I got
to join	I joined	to do	I did
to offer	I offered	to leave	I left
to want	I wanted	to fly	I flew
		to send	I sent

10.
1 am → was
2 attend → attended
3 leave → left
4 go → went
5 work → worked
6 return → returned
7 worked → work
8 miss → missed

Unit 10

1.
1 T 2 F 3 T 4 F 5 T 6 T

2.
1 words   6 Fourthly
2 aim   7 fifth
3 item   8 business
4 Under   9 AOB
5 Then   10 start

3.
1 It gives all the details of the hotel chains and the names and locations of the individual hotels.
2 Because he has been working on the new audit documents.
3 All travel costs to and from the hotels and reasonable expenses in the hotels – accommodation, drinks, meals, and so on.
4 They try to make the hotels fit into the auditors' existing work schedules.
5 A new and very exciting development they are planning for the summer.

4.
1 O   5 C   9 C
2 C   6 C   10 C
3 C   7 O
4 O   8 O

5.
1 through   3 covered   5 lengthy
2 summarize 4 Firstly   6 finally

8.
1 cleared up   3 go through
2 take up   4 tie up

Unit 11

1.
1 technological → technical
2 listen to → hear
3 possibly → quality
4 England → Italy
5 of → about
6 for → with
7 Anything → Everything
8 all → any
9 take → make

2.
1 c   2 b   3 d   4 a

3.
Sentences that don't make sense: 1, 4, 6

4.
1 The sound is OK and the picture quality is fine as well.
2 The sound here is a bit faint but the picture is clear.
3 There's no problem with the sound and the picture is clear.
4 The sound is a bit delayed and the picture is dark.
5 I can't see you but the sound is perfect.
6 The sound is a bit crackly so I miss every other word.

5.
Things that Natasha does: 1, 3, 4, 5, 7

6.
1 interrupt   3 one   5 alternative
2 hand   4 positive 6 opinion

8.
1 Is, working   4 is
2 have, met   5 didn't, come
3 are, having

9.
Correct order: i, d, h, a, f, b, j, c, e, g

Unit 12

1.
Informal words/phrases in Natasha's email:
Hi everybody
Sorry for being a bit late
I was snowed under
It's shaping up well
I can't wait to hear your 'constructive' criticism!
Honest!!
Does anybody have a problem with that?
Just give me a bell
OK
See you all
Cheers

2.
1 Does anybody have a problem with that?
2 I was snowed under
3 Sorry for being a bit late
4 I can't wait to hear your 'constructive' criticism!
5 Hi everybody
6 Cheers
7 Just give me a bell
8 See you all
9 It's shaping up well

5.
1 N 2 N 3 N, S, R 4 S 5 C

6.
Expressions used: 1, 2, 4, 5, 6, 8

7.
1 Let's not go into that now.
2 We'll come on to that later.
3 I don't want to get sidetracked at this stage.
4 Can we discuss that later please?
5 I don't want to get off the point.
6 Let's stick to the logo at the moment if we can.

8.
1 c   2 e   3 b   4 f   5 a   6 d

9.
1 opinion   4 ahead
2 think   5 about
3 suggestion   6 recommend

11.
1 I fully accept your point of view.
2 I'm completely against changing the logo.
3 I think the strategy is absolutely ridiculous.
4 I strongly recommend it.
5 The meeting went very well.

Unit 13

1.
1 Because the economic situation is terrible.
2 They are 30% down on the same time last year.
3 The forecast for the next quarter is even worse.
4 He is very worried.

2.
1 e   2 c   3 b   4 a   5 d

3.
1 firm proposal   6 small misunderstanding
2 decisive action   7 completely against
3 normal meeting   8 completely straight
4 in secret   9 effective meetings
5 rubber stamp

4.
1 f   2 e   3 b   4 a   5 d   6 c

5.
1 I think we're wasting our time talking like this.
2 I strongly believe in having effective meetings.
3 I'm not convinced that you are being completely straight with us!
4 We need to take decisive action immediately.
5 This isn't the first time we've had this sort of problem.

6.
1 T   3 F   5 F   7 F
2 T   4 T   6 T

Answer key

7.
| 1 B | 3 B | 5 A | 7 A | 9 K |
| 2 K | 4 J | 6 B | 8 M | |

8.
Number of American employees: 55
Job titles: engineers and managers
Length of contracts: 3–4 years
Accommodation: luxury apartments in the city centre
Russian staff supporting each American: a personal driver and an interpreter
Number of redundancies: between 30 and 40

11.
1. They have done a good job.
2. He has had difficulties adapting to the Russian way of life.
3. We have not visited the American office.
4. They have decided to sack a lot of workers.
5. The American engineers have lived in Russia for several years.

Unit 14

1.
Karl's relationship with the staff is informal. The greeting ('Hi everybody') and the end of the letter ('…have a good week!') are informal. He also mentions the weather and the visit from his wife.

3.
They react negatively and angrily, particularly to the company's treatment of the Russian employees.

4.
| 1 AD | 3 SP | 5 TD | 7 AD |
| 2 TD | 4 AD | 6 AD | 8 TD |

5.
1. Shall we try and focus on the positive points?
2. Looking at this positively, you've already achieved your main objective.
3. You can look at it in two ways.

6.
| 1 reaction | 3 come | 5 thoughts |
| 2 start | 4 think | |

8.
| 1 b | 2 c | 3 d | 4 a |

9.
1 cutting back	5 get back
2 get in	6 draw up
3 sort out	7 go over
4 come up	8 tie up

12.
| 1 to | 3 over | 5 to |
| 2 in | 4 back | 6 to |

Unit 15

1.
1. Seven people.

2. He wants the team to brainstorm ideas for the new Sanita website.
3. In the seminar room on Tuesday morning from 9.30 to 11.30.
4. Make sure they are familiar with the old Sanita website.

2.
Features discussed in the following order:
1. Hospitals
2. Care homes
3. Health insurance
4. Telephone advice
5. Online health information
6. Health check
7. Children's nurseries
8. Children's hospitals
9. Dental service
10. Price of membership

3.
1. So to clarify, we need to highlight the wide range of services.
2. Here's what we've come up with so far.
3. I'll just run through what we've suggested so far.

5.
| 1 b | 2 c | 3 a | 4 e | 5 d |

7.
1. I think it sounds too clinical
2. shall we have another go at pooling our ideas?
3. I'm really not convinced by that argument
4. I agree completely
5. I'd like to come in here
6. I suggest we come back to this later on
7. I think Sheila has a good point
8. Can you tell me your views on the suggested new logo for Sanita?

9.
1. I'll just summarize the discussion.
2. I'll just go through the advantages and disadvantages of the proposal.
3. I'll just clarify that point.
4. I'll just say the main points again.

Unit 16

1.
1. Bill and Sandra's relationship is more informal than formal. Although they write 'Dear' (usually more formal) at the beginning of their emails, they are on first name terms and the messages finish in a friendly way ('Best regards/wishes', 'See you on Tuesday', etc).
2. At the Sanita office.
3. Sandra, and people from the IT and marketing departments.
4. Because he doesn't want any technical problems (hitches) on the day – if he has his own equipment he will know how to use it.

2.
| 1 F | 2 T | 3 T | 4 T | 5 F | 6 F |

3.
Correct order: b, d, f, e, a, c

4.
According to Bill's description:
- the 'no claims bonus' should say 50% (not 45%)
- there should be no link to 'Products and services'
- there should be ten reasons for joining Sanita (not five)
- there should be no 'Settings' section (Hospitals, Care homes, Dental care) at all.

5.
| 1 run | 3 trying | 5 put |
| 2 a little bit | 4 over | 6 clarify |

8.
| 1 Up | 3 Up | 5 Down |
| 2 Down | 4 Up | 6 Up |

9.
1 spent	4 Did, want
2 decided, contained	5 didn't, agree
3 thought, was	

Unit 17

1.
Correct order of pictures: a, b, c

2.
1. T
2. F (they are only ideas – none have been contracted yet)
3. F (30 minutes)
4. F (the end of January)
5. F (the viewers are interested in them, not the directors)
6. T
7. F (the house is in the south of England)
8. T
9. T
10. F (the museum is near Birmingham)

3.
1 main	5 research
2 summarize	6 approval
3 projects	7 answer
4 documentary	8 last

4.
1. We've decided to produce three documentaries.
2. I think that covers the main points that have been decided.
3. I confirm that we want to make a film about Rudyard Kipling.
4. It seems that we are all decided to make a documentary about weddings.
5. Just to confirm, the documentary will be 30 minutes long.
6. I think that covers the main points of our discussion.

7 So you'll do the research by the end of the month?

5.
1 She wants to talk about accommodation and travel expenses for the camera crews.
2 Because he wants to do it by email.
3 Another videoconference.
4 Because of the time difference.

7.
1 If we want to film there, we'll need to get permission. / If we wanted to film there, we'd need to get permission.
2 If I meet them, I'll try to persuade them. / If I met them, I'd try to persuade them.
3 If we can manage it, that will look really spectacular. / If we could manage it, that would look really spectacular.
4 If they don't give their approval, the filming will have to take place somewhere else. / If they didn't give their approval, the filming would have to take place somewhere else.

10.
1 review   3 discussion 5 evaluate
2 eloquent 4 achieved   6 determine

Unit 18

1.
1 At the Move It head office in Milan.
2 Because they need to vote on several issues which affect the future development of the company.
3 So that she can inform the hotel of approximate arrival times.
4 Yes, because they will have the papers three weeks before the meeting.

2.
1 minutes   5 apologies
2 quorum   6 items arising
3 deadline   7 proxy votes
4 action points

3.
They are discussing item 4 (Acceptance or rejection of applications).

4.
1 b 2 e 3 d 4 a 5 c

5.
1 About **time** = c
2 get **round** to = f
3 a smart **cookie** = d
4 **Yeah** = a
5 **whopping** great = e
6 **sure** = b

Thomas' informal language is very inappropriate for a board meeting. In this type of meeting, participants are expected to speak and behave formally.

6.
1 reject   6 abstentions
2 point of order 7 amendment
3 objections   8 split
4 seconder   9 casting
5 put the motion

8.
1 will be held   4 had been discussed
2 was carried   5 is covered
3 has been decided

Unit 19

4.
For Kim Li, it is most important to write the minutes carefully and accurately.
For Serge Kohler, it is most important to write and circulate the minutes straight after the meeting.
For Laura Bortellotti, it is most important that the minutes are positive and don't embarrass anyone.

5.
1 time   5 reached   9 distributed
2 held   6 were   10 all
3 present   7 each   11 details
4 was   8 deadlines

6.
Questions not answered in the minutes: 3, 6, 7, 8, 9, 10

7.
1 All of them.
2 A problem with the new warehouse.
3 Because they were not strong enough financially.
4 By renting additional space in the area.

8.
1 suggested   5 decided
2 complained   6 raised
3 reported   7 explained
4 asked   8 agreed

Infinitive form of the verbs in bold: bring up, recommend, discuss, emphasize, promise, stress

9.
1 syllable: asked, raised, stressed
2 syllables: a<u>greed</u>, brought <u>up</u>, com<u>plained</u>, dis<u>cussed</u>, ex<u>plained</u>, <u>prom</u>ised
3 syllables: de<u>cid</u>ed, <u>em</u>phasized, re<u>por</u>ted, <u>sug</u>gested
4 syllables: recom<u>men</u>ded

10.
(Suggested answers)
1 He promised that everyone would have an increase in salary the following month.
2 He emphasized that the quality of the product was excellent.
3 He suggested discussing it under AOB.
4 He stressed that the project should be completed by the following week at the latest.
5 He complained that a lot of colleagues were not fully committed to the project.

Unit 20

1.
1 17th May   3 30th June 5 30th June
2 30th May   4 15th June

2.
1 e 2 d 3 b 4 a 5 c

3.

Action point	Responsible person(s)	Deadline
1 Research unusual situations for weddings	Veronica	End of January
2 Get permission to film in Rudyard Kipling's home	Veronica	End of next week
3 Check that the Black Country Museum will give permission for filming	Veronica	No date

4.
1 Formal   4 Informal 7 Formal
2 Formal   5 Informal
3 Informal 6 Formal

5.
1 T 2 F 3 F 4 T 5 T

6.
1 Karla 2 Karla 3 Moto 4 Sylvie

10.
1 the most welcoming
2 the most effective
3 clearer
4 more detailed
5 the worst
6 the best
7 longer
8 the most positive

Can do checklist

Tick (✓) all of the following statements that are true for you. For any that you cannot tick, study the relevant unit until you are able to tick it.

I can…

…tell the difference between, and talk about, different types of meetings. (Unit 1) ☐

…take part in a conversation to arrange a meeting. (Unit 2) ☐

…read and write emails in preparation for a meeting. (Unit 3) ☐

…confirm and reschedule meetings verbally and in writing. (Unit 4) ☐

…book a room or business centre for a meeting. (Unit 5) ☐

…plan and make informed decisions about a meeting. (Unit 6) ☐

…socialize with other participants before a meeting. (Unit 7) ☐

…open a meeting and get the attention of the participants. (Unit 8) ☐

…introduce myself at a meeting and talk about my background. (Unit 9) ☐

…move through a meeting agenda and summarize what has been discussed. (Unit 10) ☐

…set up a videoconference and establish ground rules. (Unit 11) ☐

…handle distractions and keep a discussion moving in the right direction. (Unit 12) ☐

…deal with strong disagreement and conflict. (Unit 13) ☐

…deal fairly and sensitively with difficult issues. (Unit 14) ☐

…understand and participate in a brainstorming meeting. (Unit 15) ☐

…make a presentation to a client about work completed. (Unit 16) ☐

…end a meeting on time and in a satisfactory way. (Unit 17) ☐

…adjust my language and behaviour to take part in a formal meeting. (Unit 18) ☐

…understand and write useful, effective minutes. (Unit 19) ☐

…monitor action and evaluate my performance in meetings. (Unit 20) ☐